AGAINST
ALL
ODDS

A DESPERATE PLEA FOR
HUMAN CONNECTION

CAROLA HAUER, PHD

This book is dedicated with tremendous gratitude to my good friends, mentors, teachers, and spirit guides

Without their amazing encouragement, support, and faith in me, I could not have completed this book

TABLE OF CONTENTS

A history of adverse childhood experiences stands in a survivor's way, often for a lifetime, no matter how much healing work they might do. History has shown that unfortunately, people who experienced traumatic upbringings are generally considered as less than those who have not, and too often they are no longer considered to be credible, especially when it comes to legal matters.

Medical procedures can be extremely retraumatizing for complex trauma survivors, and trauma-informed care can make an amazing difference for them. When a survivor is believed, understood, and met with even a bit of compassion by those they come in contact with, there is often a better treatment outcome.

Listening, believing, and staying open-minded are the most important attitudes toward any complex trauma survivor and can make an amazing difference, especially when that individual is in crisis. We will never know how much utter despair the person experiences, how vulnerable and overwhelmed the person feels, if he or she has reached the end of their rope, or perhaps struggles with the decision whether to try to stay alive or to follow the urge to die.

Part 2

Defining and understanding trauma is not an easy task. Each trauma is an incredibly unique and individual matter, yet there are also universal patterns and experiences to reckon with. Therefore, the survivor and his or her support system may find themselves confronted by unexpected obstacles, which so often are present in the complex landscape that each journey presents.

Just like the stages of grief, the stages of trauma recovery do not show up in any logical order, because they often have a life of their own. Therefore, the stages of trauma recovery, especially for complex trauma survivors may overlap or show up in a bizarre order and may be confusing to everybody involved.

The effects of adverse childhood experiences are vast and long-lasting and unfortunately there is still truly little known and understood about the topic. The most important takeaway is that we simply cannot just snap out of it, and it takes time and adequate help to facilitate healing.

When the traumatic brain gets triggered, meaning the survivor is dealing with a real or perceived threat, the main focus in the brain is on survival, meaning there is a limited ability for the survivor to access the rational part of the brain and the executive functions of the brain.

Traumatic memory is stored in a number of different areas of the brain and various aspects of memory are often somewhat disconnected. Survivors may have difficulty bringing certain information forward at times, yet research has shown that the information in regard to their trauma itself, is in general fairly accurate.

Chapter 9: Trauma and Dissociation 69
Dissociation is a healthy and natural coping mechanism but when overused, it also creates its own sets of problems, meaning while detaching oneself from the life experiences on the outside (because that is often literally the only way to survive horrific torture and abuse) it can also interfere with the post-trauma life, especially when it comes to interpersonal relationships.

Chapter 10: Trauma and Addiction 75
While an Adverse Childhood Experiences (or ACEs) score of four and above increases the likelihood for addiction exponentially, an ACEs score of six and above causes even more destruction and often leads to IV drug use. Over 80 percent of addicts report having significant adverse childhood experiences, which means that mental health treatment, in general, needs to focus on co-occurring disorders, and that we all need to be more involved in preventing adverse childhood experiences overall.

Chapter 11: The Internal Self-Care System 81
Since dissociation is a way to detach from the self, it makes sense that survivors end up with a number of fragmented or detached parts of the self. Complex trauma survivors have an internal system in place that may step in when a threat is experienced or perceived, and shift into complete survival mode. The general goal is to escape the overwhelming pain, which at times may be warranted or unwarranted, may lead to self-destructive behaviors, and in extreme cases could even lead to suicide.

Chapter 12: Learning from Human Experience. 85
As the most developed species on this planet, humans not only have the most developed brain capacity—and with that the most developed set of tools—but humans are also very sophisticated and have defense mechanisms in place, such as denial, doubt, and

arrogance, that can get into the way of learning from another person's trauma. Therefore, humans can easily assume that what happened to another person will not happen to them and with that, they can miss great opportunities to learn from each other.

Part 3

Part 4

The Myth of Inanna can be used rather effectively as a type of road map to gain some understanding and insight into the challenging journey toward healing for a complex trauma survivor. Like many other myths, it can help survivors and their support alike to understand the journey into the underworld, how to best support each other, and what to expect along the way.

Unless we open our hearts to each other and especially to ourselves, true healing cannot take place. Complex trauma survivor's sense of self has most likely been shattered by the original trauma and the negative messages given to them relentlessly have taken residency on the inside of the survivors. They cannot see anything remotely good about themselves, which hinders true healing.

Together we can break those chains that have kept complex trauma survivors in their own universe. Re-entry into society is not a small task, and complex trauma survivors need all the support they can get to make the transition from living in survival mode twenty-four-seven into a more fulfilling and peaceful life.

FOREWORD

THIS BOOK IS DEDICATED TO all those who have been suffering, are currently suffering, or will be suffering from complex trauma so often caused by heinous and unspeakable childhood abuse. Though for many of us the original abuse may lie in the past, most of us, no matter what age, are still dealing with the aftermath of what we lived through to some degree or another. When I finally began my personal therapy, I realized that the long-term consequences of my own trauma had been overshadowing every aspect of my adult life causing me to suffer for way too long. They kept me doubting, judging, and mistrusting myself for as long as I could remember. Most of all, they made me feel like I did not have a real purpose in my life, other than being the target for abuse. When I grasped that I am truly not alone and that millions of other survivors struggled with very similar life-long pain, I felt somehow, I had to find a way to write about this topic.

The reason I am sharing part of my narrative and why I have invited others to share parts of their narrative, is because our goal is to give voice to the overwhelming pain we have lived through and are still living through. We want to encourage those who are on their way to recovery, and help educate our support systems and those who might be interested in learning about our unique challenges. It is our collective desire to instill hope, make our difficult journey better understood, reduce unnecessary retraumatization, and witness that faint glimmer of hope (which many of us have felt from time to time) that our life not yet lived is truly worth fighting for.

My intention is also to acknowledge and honor those who, sadly, ended up taking their own lives either early on or later into the difficult journey of their recovery. Too often they are judged as having committed "the most *selfish* act one could ever commit," which to me is incredibly dismissive. It lacks any form of understanding or compassion, and shows that many of us remain utterly misunderstood, even into our death. I wish, as a society, we would acknowledge those tremendous losses instead of making up all sorts of excuses for their deaths. Perhaps we could make a difference for those who are wavering and are contemplating taking their own life today and with that, prevent family members and friends from losing a loved one to suicide, which leaves the survivors not only marked by deep sadness and grief, but also at a higher risk of considering taking their own life.

Interestingly enough, *selfish* according to Merriam-Webster is an adjective that describes someone "lacking any consideration for others, someone who is excessively and exclusively concerned with his or her own advantage, personal profit, or pleasure." I firmly believe that anyone who intentionally harms another person, especially a totally innocent child, might deserve such a label. I also firmly believe that his or her victim truly does not deserve such a label. Perhaps we could simply acknowledge that the victimized individual may have felt too broken or too defeated to go on.

While I am personally and professionally fighting to help people stay alive, I can honestly say that I can relate on the deepest level to the feelings of total defeat and utter desperation. Patients have often asked me if have ever been in such a dark place where I had personally contemplated taking my own life, especially if I met them after a suicide attempt. I would answer their question honestly and share with them that I struggled with suicidality for a big portion of my life. Then I would share with them how grateful I was to still be alive. Just that bit of transparency not only helped create rapport, but it made patients feel understood, knowing they were talking to someone who was not going to judge them harshly. Many times I was told, after such an honest and sacred encounter, that the mere fact that I was where I was, not only inspired them, but also gave them more hope for their own journey.

I am extremely grateful for the opportunities I have had, and still have, to serve in the mental-health profession and for the difference that I have been able to make with God's help and the help of so many others. Yet I am also keenly aware that there is so much more that needs to be done. I so wish that adverse childhood experiences were a thing of the past, but unfortunately it is not the case. In fact, I believe with many other professionals that adverse childhood experiences may just be our biggest public health crisis, and it is truly begging to be addressed with boldness and honesty.

It is rather heartbreaking knowing that the SARS-CoV-2 pandemic led to an increase in child abuse and domestic violence, and that violent family disturbances have significantly increased in numbers, especially while we were on lockdown. There were no teachers, nurses, or school psychologists who would have been able to identify cases and involve child protective services and law enforcement, because kids were not in school. They would not be seen regularly by doctors or any other emergency medical personnel. Every medical facility was either shut down or completely overwhelmed by Covid cases.

It will take time to understand the impact and the magnitude of what happened behind closed doors. Whole families were completely isolated and did not have any outlets to deal effectively with the stressors of everyday life and the negative emotions that follow. Even domestic violence shelters and transitional housing had to shut down during the lockdown, due to the recommended restrictions, and that unfortunately does not mean people were any safer during those times. There are enough reports that have already provided statistics showing these incidents increased instead of decreased, as one would hope. To me, the sad part is that there was not much any of us could do to hold people accountable or to intervene, and I feel a sense of responsibility to bring some awareness to that abuse, as well. If we all could stay more attuned to these delicate issues, I believe together we can all make a difference and hopefully help some survivors of complex trauma, who completely feel alone and misunderstood, and too many of them are suffering in silence.

INTRODUCTION

MY PERSONAL TRAUMA BEGAN WHEN I was born into post-war Germany, with its Nazi-era residue. An environment that was not just laden with a dire political climate, but one that also created toxic family dynamics and negatively infiltrated the fiber of society overall. My life was grossly overshadowed by adverse childhood experiences from birth until I turned eighteen. These included physical, sexual, emotional, and verbal abuse as well as neglect, family dysfunction, domestic violence, divorce, mental-health issues, and substance abuse. My abuse was perpetrated by my caretakers, their associates, and even complete strangers outside our smaller circle. These perpetrators shared two key things: free access to myself as well as countless other defenseless children all around me, and the opportunity to get away with their horrific behaviors.

When I finally sought professional help, after I had immigrated to the United States from Germany in 1985, my first psychologist—in one of our very first sessions—said, "With most patients, we can just go into the mind and remove a traumatic event, like a slice of their life, and they will be able to heal and go on. If we used that approach with you, we would have to erase your whole childhood and all of your teenage years. There would be nothing left."

His analysis left me rightfully confused and wondering if there was any way for me to ever fully heal; nevertheless, at least I knew I had taken a step in the right direction. A step that definitely marked the beginning of my journey toward healing and a better life.

That was decades ago, and so much has changed in the treatment of complex trauma by now. I am sure I am not the only veteran survivor who ended up in basic treatment for depression, anxiety, and some form of PTSD, which did not address the more complex and longer-lasting issues of the trauma. Because our trauma originated so early in our childhood and was marked by such a

1

significant level of betrayal, it impacted all of our developmental years; therefore, there are additional psychological components to address. With what I was able to access during the late eighties and throughout the nineties, my life did not become perfect by any means. It was a start, and it helped me to tap into a level of inner peace I had never imagined possible. It changed my life so significantly. I knew there were hundreds and thousands of individuals out there who were suffering as badly as I had, or worse, and I decided to go back to school and pursue my education in clinical psychology.

It was so liberating for me to discover I was actually neither crazy, nor weird and/or defective, but that the sheer dynamics of my complex trauma and its long-term consequences had been dictating all my post-trauma adult life. It finally made sense to me at times when my original trauma was triggered, I'd be completely overwhelmed by some simple events in everyday life. Being triggered made me default to using my old coping mechanisms, causing me to fall into old habits and behaviors automatically. Learning about my trauma and how it continued to impact me even years later enabled me to no longer look at myself as too broken, too damaged, or simply not good enough. Instead, I realized what I had experienced was not as unusual as I had thought, and I was not a "bad person," "crazy," or "abnormal." I learned that the prolonged adverse childhood experiences originated with "abnormal people," shaping my whole life very negatively. I also learned that I responded in the best way I could at the time with the tools I had available as a young child and teenager. Gaining that insight allowed me to slowly develop a sense of gratitude toward myself.

My healing journey was not only difficult, but it was also a long and drawn-out process. Looking back, I can clearly see when I began my studies in psychology, I had only partially healed. It took years for me to stop being my own worst enemy and to develop a level of understanding and empathy for the complex dynamics embedded in my psyche. It was still much easier for me to have compassion for others, especially other trauma survivors, than it was for me to develop any level of compassion for *myself*, a well-known

2

issue for any of us who survived such pervasive trauma so early in our lives. It was much easier for me to look out for those I worked with than it was for me to recognize I also needed to protect myself.

I was told every day that I was "stupid" or a "liar" or that "I did not amount to anything worthwhile," therefore, I ended up internalizing these negative messages, and I could not see anything positive in myself. My negative self-talk became woven into the fabric of my life. I had to reprogram, believe in myself, and learn to generate more positive self-talk. I neither had the insight nor the mental capacity to understand the maltreatment I had survived. I had to understand what took place had not been my fault, and it took years of treatment for me to finally see things more objectively.

Furthermore, I had to learn to understand how simple everyday situations triggered me and why, and how to work with these situations in a more effective way. Until I received treatment, I could not apply anything else but my "black-and-white thinking" or assess even minor setbacks or difficulties as matters of "life and death." When I eventually began understanding my triggers, that did not necessarily mean I was able to cope with them any better. But it taught me to shift into damage control before reacting, and I gradually learned how to postpone my traumatic reactions.

In the process of my personal therapy and my professional studies I learned our clinical picture and presentation is like that of other trauma survivors with Post-Traumatic Stress Disorder (PTSD) and that there are also significant differences between the two. We do share classic symptoms of PTSD, including reliving the original trauma or experiencing flashbacks, having to avoid situations that may trigger past traumatic events, not trusting our surroundings, and not feeling safe in the world. But our condition poses additional challenges, because our abuse was prolonged, premeditated, and usually inflicted by a caretaker or a trusted family member. Since our trauma overshadows our developmental years, we often end up with an extreme negative self-view, which often makes us feel different from everybody else. We usually have difficulty regulating sudden strong emotions, we may create or stay in unhealthy relationships. Too often we feel completely detached from ourselves, including our emotions or our physical sensations or both.

Bessel van der Kolk, in the book *The Body keeps the Score*, makes so many excellent points, writing about survivors of complex trauma. When I read his statement "that complex trauma survivors basically live in a different universe until they have had a chance to do some healing work," it really resonated with me—because that is how it felt—and it allowed me to feel relieved. I can honestly tell you that nothing made any sense to me while I was growing up. If anybody asks me what I learned during those years, the answer is: how to survive ... Survival 101, 102, and 103 ... that is it. I felt completely alone because I could not imagine another human being might be going through anything like what I was experiencing. I grew up feeling flawed and became convinced over time there must be something inherently wrong with me or I would not have ended up in my situation. So, needless to say, I was nowhere close to being ready for life when I turned eighteen.

I managed to survive my abusive circumstances by mentally detaching myself from my traumatic experiences. I had to develop strong dissociative defense mechanisms, and ended up with a fractured psyche. I simply developed distinct aspects of myself, which at times took over to help my core deal with the complete overwhelm. It made it possible for me to get away from my emotional pain, at least internally. I believe this dynamic explains why so many of us can present as extremely strong and at other times we can be extremely sensitive. Why we can sometimes present as mature and at other times make immature decisions. We can be loving and at the same time get agitated, which gets rather confusing for everyone involved—including us.

It was powerful for me to discover that the psychological community has learned over time, unless the therapeutic approach focuses on paying attention to all parts of a complex trauma survivor, including their despised, disowned, and dissociated parts, survivors of complex trauma cannot put all their pieces back together. This means unless we as survivors can give voice to all our parts and resolve the conflict between them, we will continue with our daily struggles. Often including self-harm, addiction, and other self-destructive behaviors. Like many defensive mechanisms, preservative and protective at one time, if held too long in one place, they take on their own life and their own rhythms and create their own problems. We may default to that behavior anytime we sense a threat in our environment. It takes tremendous courage on the part of the survivor and tremendous skill and caring on the part of the professional, to help heal the severe fragmentation on the inside of the survivor and help invite the psyche back into wholeness (Fisher, 2021).

I speak for many complex trauma survivors when I say we cannot wait to learn how to undo these defensive mechanisms, on our way to wholeness, so we can regain a sense of control in our post-trauma life and only use these mechanisms when absolutely necessary. Imagine how surprised we survivors are to find ourselves triggered by some random everyday event, even after years of therapy, suddenly and unexpectedly causing us to panic, rendering us completely vulnerable, and kicking our old coping mechanisms right back into high gear. As you can see, our process of recovery is not linear but complex like our original trauma. It is only human that we will make some progress and take a few steps back. Rest assured, we are usually the ones who feel the most disappointed and discouraged by our behavior.

When our trauma gets triggered, all we can really do is work on calming our internal system and regaining our composure as quickly as we can. Once we have gotten a hold of ourselves on the inside, we can then try to assess the collateral damage on the outside. If our internal self-care system deployed our dissociative defenses, we may have already detached from our immediate surroundings and negative experiences. It may take us days or even weeks to wrap our heads around what triggered our trauma responses and why. These experiences are not only disheartening, but they can set us back significantly. They often make us realize though we did tremendous work in our recovery and met our challenges head on, our specific issues still prevail in one form or another and may prevail for as long as we live.

Being randomly triggered, as a complex trauma survivor, often takes us back to our original trauma. This can leave us in a vulnerable place, because it can still elicit painful memories and create some default behaviors. It is something we just have to deal with. It is even more disheartening when we have to deal with completely avoidable triggers, meaning situations in everyday life, that could have been handled in a much more compassionate way. These "avoidable" situations occur because society still has such limited understanding of mental health and even more difficulty dealing with us as complex trauma survivors and with how we present in the world. Therefore, my goal is to help educate the reader about the recovery from complex trauma so we can hopefully be better understood and better supported. I want to help demystify our trauma reactions and explain what we are trying to do is to manage our strong emotions. Just a bit of understanding and compassion goes a long way.

See, when we survivors get triggered, we often end up feeling shamed, embarrassed, dismissed, vulnerable, exploited, and at a complete loss—especially if we shift into fight, flight, or freeze responses—and we may become short-tempered, irritable, or even aggressive. It may make us check out completely, depending on our automatic responses to certain stressors. Likewise, when family members or supporters get triggered, they often feel similarly embarrassed, confused, or even overwhelmed, and they might take our trauma reactions personally and feel a need to engage their own defenses. Misunderstandings and misinterpretations play a key role in these situations, and if we could work together on increasing understanding, empathy, and compassion, we would feel equally respected, cared for, and understood.

Non-survivors, individuals who did not have to endure and suffer through complex trauma, in general have a tough time relating, understandably so; therefore, their ability to deal with even a fraction of our narrative often frightens them and is too painful for them. My objective is to share, articulate, educate, and shed light onto the issue of complex trauma in a way that makes sense and also allows the reader to remain present, reflect more deeply, be better prepared, become more thoughtful and understanding, and act more tactfully and thoughtfully in any given situation. I believe, in general, non-survivors do not want to make our lives any more difficult than they already are. I also believe the last thing we as survivors want to do is traumatize another innocent person around us, such as our family members, our friends, and other people. If we were all better informed and we all better understood what complex trauma is and how it impacts survivors long term, and how to respond to it more effectively, I know we would all be better able to manage crisis situations of any kind.

Unnecessary and avoidable retraumatization of complex trauma survivors are often not only damaging in the moment but can have long lasting effects that may take us to familiar dark places we have worked so hard to leave behind. Reinforcing our belief that the world will never be a safe place. I know first-hand about the importance of listening and building an alliance with the survivor as far as their treatment and even their treatment outcomes are concerned. The most important components of trauma-informed care are about establishing a sense of safety, developing trust, and creating a good understanding, as well as showing compassion and empathy. I passionately believe that if we could extend this approach to everybody we encounter, together we could make a significant difference in everyday life.

The medical community had to revamp their whole approach to patient care. It became increasingly evident that it was extremely important to factor into the medical diagnosis and treatment of every patient if they had a trauma history or not. Not only does trauma have a significant impact on physical, mental, and behavioral functioning of any individual, patients who have a trauma history may or may not respond to their treatment as expected, simply because they have difficulty dealing with the stress of a medical encounter or they have difficulty trusting the healthcare system itself. Some will go as far as saying considering a patient's past and developing trauma-informed treatment will not only improve patient care but also impact the treatment outcome. Consequently, patients who are acting outside of a "normal" response in the particular setting, are generally treated with a bit more compassion and dignity by the medical community.

There is mounting evidence, especially in the most recent decade, that trauma-informed care and mindfulness are extremely important practices. We need to stay open minded, postpone judgment, and use loving kindness and compassion as we deal with one another. Therefore, the best question to ask when encountering a situation where someone acts outside the norm is clearly not, "What is wrong with you?" Instead, it would be much more helpful to ask, "What do you need?" or "What happened?" and "How can I help?"

Trauma survivors who are being treated by others with gentle kindness and compassion and with a mindful attitude will almost always respond more positively. The difference in approach alone has an enormous impact on those of us who have been dealing with complex trauma and are still struggling with its long-term consequences. I will highlight in later chapters some firsthand experiences, which will let you see for yourself how significant the treatment outcome can be impacted by a simple shift in attitude. This is not to say that those of us who are dealing with a complex trauma history have the right to frighten others, infringe on others, or manipulate others. It is to say, though, that we do not deserve to be retraumatized by harsh judgment or by completely avoidable sequences and events.

Too many of us are, unfortunately, still met with an overall lack of understanding, tolerance, and empathy in everyday life. Some family and friends get annoyed with us because we are still dealing with issues of our past, much to their dismay. Even if we have learned to speak up and let those around us know ahead of time that we are struggling with a particular issue or procedure, too many of them still have a difficult time relating to us. Too often, as survivors of complex trauma, we are asked by those around us "why we still care," "why we have not gotten over things that are so far in the past," and "why we cannot snap out of it," which is just as disheartening to us as our reactions are to those around us. Frequently, we get accused of wanting to dwell in our misery, or we are

8

being told we are just looking for people to have pity on us. In most cases, it could not be further from the truth. In fact, the majority of complex trauma survivors want to get away from the past. Most of us have no desire to dwell in our misery. Most of us do not want any pity from anybody.

I believe the reason for such misunderstanding and misinterpretation lies in the fact that we have not shared enough of the new insights and information about recovery from complex trauma, which are available to clinicians and some of their support staff, but usually are not available to families and friends or the general public. They are the ones dealing with us most of the time in everyday life, and because a good support system is one major key to our recovery, we need to find a way to close that gap. Unfortunately, we are losing too many complex trauma survivors to suicide. Even while I authored this book, we lost a very dear friend of our family who could no longer deal with the pain she was going through. It affected so many of us very deeply, and left her immediate family completely devastated.

> The success of our lives and our future depends on our individual motivation and determination. When unfortunate things happen in our lives, there are two results. One possibility would be mental unrest, anxiety, fear, doubt, frustration, and eventually depression, and in the worst case even suicide. The other possibility would be that because of the tragic experience(s) we become more realistic. Overall, with the power of investigation, the tragic experience(s) may make us even stronger, and increase our self-esteem, our self-confidence, and our self-reliance. The unfortunate can become a source of inner strength (The Dalai Lama, 2012).

In order for us to be able to let the unfortunate become our source of inner strength, we all need to have more knowledge and a better understanding of trauma itself, have a more mindful approach to it, and gain tools that will be effective on a broader scale. As a scholar, a defender, and one of the representatives of survivors

9

of complex trauma, my deepest desire is to educate as many people as possible. Personally, I struggled with the aftermath of my trauma for decades because I did not know how to go about my recovery from my early life experiences. Somehow, I survived, and somehow, I found the strength to continue to put one foot in front of the other. I thank God for that. Looking back though, I wish I could have found the right help sooner than I did, and I can honestly say that more compassion, more understanding, and more support would have made quite a difference in my life, and in the lives of those around me.

For the above reasons, I have decided to use lived experience to highlight how these complex issues play out in our everyday life and that many of us still experience some long-term consequences from our original trauma, even though we might have already done some extensive work. I hope to bridge the gap, create more compassion, and provide some effective tools to help avoid unnecessary retraumatization of the survivor and unnecessary traumatization of the supporter or innocent bystander.

PART 1

CHAPTER 1

DAMAGED GOODS

I WAS IN A MAJOR ACCIDENT in 1994, when my car was hit by, in all probability, a drunk driver in an intersection early in the morning. I was heading to my work at a university, where I was in my master's program studying to become a Marriage and Family Therapist. By the time the car accident occurred, I had years of therapy under my belt, and I no longer had flashbacks of some of the unbelievable and unthinkable events I survived during my upbringing. For clarification, I was neither texting nor was I on my phone, nor did I pay attention to anything aside from the road. I was hit by a driver who ran a red light, I simply had no chance to avoid this accident. None of us are exempt from experiences like major car accidents, medical trauma, or even bank robberies at gunpoint for that matter. Bad things can happen to all of us. Unfortunately, it happens that those of us who have had a painful past most often are treated very differently.

The accident occurred only a few blocks from my home, where I was on route to my work in the early morning hours. It was a familiar route for me, and when I saw I had a green light, I went toward the intersection without much hesitation. Moments later, though, I noticed a white pick-up truck to my right that was not slowing down. Instead it was approaching the intersection at a high speed. The driver must have had a red light since my light was still green. This was later confirmed by a witness. I realized if the truck was not going to slow down, it was likely I would get hit. I had two choices—I could try to brake, hoping I could avoid the collision or at least reduce the impact, or I could try to position

13

my small car in a way that upon impact I would not be completely T-boned. Since there was no way for me to get my car to slow down enough to avoid the collision, I decided that I would try to maneuver my car in a way so that I would not be completely crushed by the truck, which I did. I was hit at the passenger door and the right back fender. My car flipped onto the driver's side upon impact, and due to my desperate maneuver, my car was miraculously pushed away from the truck instead. There was so much force my car ended up rolling over and tumbling in different directions. When I had lost every bit of control over my car, I placed my hands around my head for protection.

When I finally came to a stop, the engine was still running. I smelled gasoline. I heard loud and clear in my head, "Turn off your engine" ... "swing over your legs" ... "unbuckle your seatbelt" ... "get out of the car!" I followed these instructions and when I tried to reorient myself, I saw that despite the glass particles that were covering me, the front windshield had fallen out in one piece. I was literally able to walk out of my car. I was the first one to make it to the sidewalk, and I watched the driver of the truck struggle to unbuckle his seat belt. When he eventually got out of his vehicle, strangely enough, he never came closer to see if I was OK. I heard the sirens coming closer and I watched a fire truck, an ambulance, and a police car fly into the intersection. The site was pretty bad, with glass and random pieces of my mangled car thrown all over the intersection. Gasoline was leaking everywhere. It was somewhat surreal to watch the scene unfold. This was not the first time for me to be somewhat a bystander watching what just happened to me.

The firemen checked out the wreck and then contained the gasoline, which was still spilling out, while the police officer spoke to the driver of the truck, who later just drove off. I could tell that they were frantically looking for a dead or at least a severely mangled body, and eventually one of them shouted from a distance asking if I was the driver. I nodded yes. They stared at me in disbelief and a bit later asked, again from a distance, if I was OK, and this time, I just shrugged my shoulders. Nobody came to check me out closely, and because it was assumed that I was all right, it honestly did not occur to me to ask to be checked out medically. I was still in shock, I sure wish that help would have been offered to me, and I know I would not have turned it down.

The fire crew flipped my car back around, collected the salvageable items I had in the wreck, and gave them to me. They started sweeping up the debris and then dealt with the gasoline spill. I assume because I was still standing, somebody decided the ambulance could leave without me. That's when I noticed a sinking feeling in my stomach. I was not able to speak up, because mentally I had completely checked out and because I was all by myself—there was nobody there to advocate for me.

It turned out that the truck driver was a contractor on the way to his job. He called me a few days later saying something to the effect of, "I am so sorry! I thought I had killed you!" He also said something to the effect that he should not have been driving that morning, and expressed some regrets. It left me even more perplexed, and I really did not know what to do with that call. I assumed we would be communicating at some later point, little did I know that I would never see or hear from the man again. He never experienced any legal consequences, as far as I know.

I took my final exam shortly after the accident. I completely flunked, because I could neither concentrate nor recall any information. I passed my class because I had done well prior to my accident—which was later held against me as well. In fact, I could not take any classes at all for a while. I felt crowded and unsafe by the amount of people around me in my class, nor could I tolerate auditory and visual input simultaneously. I felt like jumping out of my skin because I experienced such severe anxiety, felt so confused, and was easily agitated. I relived the roller-coaster feeling over and over, meaning the sensation of my car tipping to the left, hearing the scraping noises from car parts being torn off, looking straight at the asphalt including the feeling of hanging upside down in my seat belt, and smelling gasoline, which was extremely disturbing.

Weeks later, I learned that the driver of the truck had not been insured, and that my insurance was willing to replace my totaled car. They refused to pay for any personal damages or injuries, even though I had uninsured motorist insurance and personal injury insurance. It was explained to me that I obviously did not have a case, because I had been able to "walk away" from the accident. I was told that had I been taken to the hospital, treated, and diagnosed by medical doctors following the accident, things would have been very different.

I knew I was not well, and I was struggling to understand what was happening to me. All my will power and all the chiropractic adjustments I was getting were not enough to get me to a better place. The attorney I hired to deal with my insurance eventually requested neurological testing about six months after the incident, It was determined that I had suffered a traumatic brain injury, which caused a lesion on my left temporal lobe, and that my left inner ear had been damaged in the accident as well. I also suffered a post-traumatic seizure, and I had several unexplained falls shortly after the accident. After I saw the neurologist, and after I was properly diagnosed, with help of an EEG and a few additional tests, I was finally able to grasp what I was dealing with. This was not only a big relief but also a serious step toward my recovery. Additionally, I was given biofeedback sessions, which were incredibly helpful to me and finally allowed me to somewhat feel relaxed again for the first time in six months.

As you will see later, having a proper medical diagnosis did not help me with my claim. In fact, the medical findings were never even discussed during the arbitration. I was prepared to deal with who had the green light and who had the red light, and I actually had a witness to testify for me. I was prepared to speak to the physical and psychological symptoms I was still dealing with, and I was prepared to make statements to speak about the cost I had incurred due to the accident. What I was not prepared for was that none of what I just mentioned mattered in court.

The opposing counsel had built their argument solely around the fact that I'd had a painful past. Therefore I was not a credible witness. I had shared a college paper with my therapist pertaining to my years of sexual abuse and how I had slowly conquered my long-lasting issues stemming from the ongoing injustice. Not only did all my therapy notes become public record, but the opposing counsel argued that I was not possibly "credible" because I had "prior damage." Therefore, they called me a liar and a fraud and argued that I was trying to make a quick buck off the insurance company without having a case. They went so far as to say that putting my hands over my head for protection had caused me to lose control over my car and basically cause the accident. They even argued any other "normal" person would have taken this as an "oops experience" and they would not have caused their car to get out of control, but just gone on with their regular day, unharmed. After all, their expert witness who read the record and rendered his opinion on my mental state was a high-powered neurologist. That was again acceptable to the court, though, surprisingly a psychologist had never been consulted in this case.

Why the facts about the accident were never brought to the table and why the legal system gave the opposing attorneys permission to treat me the way they did, I have no idea. The process was brutal and, as you might imagine, all I wanted to do was run after two full days of torture. My attorney begged me not to leave and explained that I would end up being in contempt of court if I did. So, the only choice I had was to sit there and take it, until I finally crumbled, ending up in a fetal position in my chair, rocking back and forth, completely dissociated. I was no longer mentally present by the time the arbitrator rendered his decision and no I longer cared about the man's opinion. He had simply allowed this "second rape" to happen in his court room. All I could think of was that I needed to find a safe way to take care of me, because I was in horrible shape. I needed to get away from the abusive situation—as quickly as I could—to somehow restore my baseline.

It took me weeks to get to a better place mentally, and I honestly had no interest in finding out what the outcome of the horrendous arbitration was. Through my attorney, I learned that the arbitrator awarded an amount the insurance company had to pay out just above what my insurance coverage had been, which legally meant that they had acted in "bad faith" and that I had a right to have an

17

additional mediation. I could not even imagine putting myself into another situation where I would be at the mercy of an arbitrator or mediator, not knowing what I would be exposed to and how much pain I would have to endure. I was assured that the next mediation would take place in a different format, where I would not have to meet with my "accusers" face-to-face. The different parties would be in different rooms. The mediator would be the one going back and forth, so I very reluctantly agreed to go through with it.

I will never forget the mediator who treated me not only with respect but who clearly had some compassion, and who had actually taken the time to study the case in depth without charging me $450 per hour like the opposing counsel's neurologist did. The mediator went back and forth between the rooms, and after a while he reported to us that the representatives of the insurance company were already expressing how embarrassed they felt by the tiny amount they had been allotted for the purpose of this mediation. Apparently, the mediator had asked them what they thought gave them the right to treat an obviously high-functioning, decent person that way, and they could not come up with a reasonable answer.

At the end of the arbitration, I was asked if I wanted to speak to the insurance representatives before leaving the meeting. I took the opportunity because I was hoping that voicing my perspective of this brutal experience could perhaps make a slight difference for other survivors who may find themselves in a similar situation. I urged them to carefully consider how they were going to treat the next innocent person who had already endured so many wrongs in their life. They did not deserve to be re-abused, only because somebody happened to run a red light and, in the process, almost killed them. I could not really gauge if they were sincere, though they all had tears in their eyes when I was done speaking. I chose to give them the benefit of the doubt, just like they should have given me.

REFLECTIONS

The attorneys apparently felt they had the right to dig around in my painful past, which had little to nothing to do with the uninsured motorist who ran a red light and hit my car so hard that it flipped through the intersection like I was on a rollercoaster ride and almost killed me. I am certain they will never know, or care to know for that matter, what painful memories the aftermath of this horrific arbitration brought up for me, because they don't have a reason to ever look back. But for me, things took a different turn, because a contractor with an altered mental status in the early morning hours, who behaved in such a bizarre way to a serious car accident, which he obviously caused, is not an unfamiliar sight for me.

Truth be told, I grew up with a horribly abusive stepfather who was a truck driver and a serious alcoholic. He would also be dressed in overalls, and be impaired by the time 6:30 a.m. rolled around, just like the driver who ran the red light in the early morning hours in March of 1994. See, I became my stepfather's co-pilot on days I did not have school, from about ages six to eighteen, because I was clearly a burden to the "family" and was informed that I needed to earn my keep. My workday started at about 4 a.m. and lasted until about 2 p.m., and I was tasked with having to purchase the liquor for the day. But my main job as co-pilot was to make sure that my driver stayed awake while driving his truck at least five times the size of the truck that hit me by running the red light. Since my driver was drinking alcohol from the moment we started our shift, he often drove erratically or at times he slumped into his seat, drifting off while he was maneuvering this huge truck through dense traffic in the city of Berlin.

Red lights were especially tricky, because the pause in activity frequently caused him to literally fall asleep. The man proudly told me that he had assaulted a police officer with a sledgehammer once, who came to check on him because he had fallen asleep at a red light, and his truck was blocking the intersection when the light turned green. The assault bought him a brief time in jail, but it was clear to me that my stepfather had absolutely no remorse and felt he had done nothing wrong. That same sledgehammer was still behind his driver's seat, and because I knew that this man was capable of much more violence than hitting a police officer in the head, I was trying to do everything in my power to avoid such an incident. I was terrified.

On numerous occasions, I screamed my lungs out trying to wake him up, upon which he would either start driving, or quickly correct the speed or the trajectory of the gigantic truck, and we were able to avoid a number of major accidents. So, being accused of supposedly having caused the accident in 1994 did not sit well with me because I knew better, after having been in charge of a huge truck at such an early age. I clearly understand the difference between a red and green light. See, if my driver felt I did not wake him up in time or that I put him under undue pressure, or if he felt I read the traffic light or traffic signs incorrectly, he held *me* responsible. The punishment was that he either screamed at me and threatened violent acts towards me, or I ended up getting a serious beating—right then and there. So, if you wonder if I still pay attention to green and red lights and if I am trying to avoid any type of accident, the answer is *yes*, I do.

I do not believe my complete, personal history needed to be unveiled and made public, and I believe I did not deserve to be treated as someone who was not credible, simply because I suffered serious trauma in the past—but unfortunately, this is how our legal system works. As a front-line worker, I understand that in a crisis situation, we absolutely do not have the right to share detailed information about anybody or anything that does not pertain to the emergent situation in front of us. There are things that should remain private, and the person who experiences the crisis or the traumatic events should determine what he or she is willing or ready to share. Everybody has the right to privacy, and everybody deserves to be treated with dignity and respect, especially in a crisis situation and in a court of law. As a professional, it is my legal and ethical obligation to protect my patients and not expose them to exploitation, scrutiny, and embarrassment. I feel this obligation should be shared by those who represent us in our government as well as those who work within the court of law.

These are daily occurrences for complex trauma survivors when dealing with certain institutions, such as law enforcement and the legal system. It is my opinion that it is absolutely time for serious reviews and serious corrections, and for the implementation of trauma-informed care everywhere. To this day, we are being discriminated against and discredited, simply because we have had a painful past.

So, on one hand, we are told that our abuse happened so long ago that we need to be over it by now and there is something wrong with us if we are still dealing with any aspects of our trauma. On the other hand, anytime anything happens to us where we need help, such as after an accident or in another serious crisis situation, we are deemed as not credible because of our past trauma. The same people that argue one way in one incident will argue the complete opposite way in another incident, as long as it serves them. So, my question is, which one is it? Are there long-term consequences for complex trauma survivors or not? If so, wouldn't it make sense that we all educate ourselves about it and develop some kind of understanding and perhaps develop some sense of compassion?

CHAPTER 2

TRAUMA INFORMED CARE ... OR NOT

HERE IS ANOTHER PERSONAL EXAMPLE highlighting how trauma-informed care can help and what its absence can cause. For this purpose, I will share with you two of my most recent surgeries, which turned out very differently. I always alert my medical team of my condition without giving them a sob story because first, I want to spare myself from as many negative experiences as I can, and second, I want to spare others from having to deal with any type of fallout, which often is more than just embarrassing.

In 2009, I had to undergo a life-saving surgery. My surgeon was clearly puzzled how I could be so calm in the face of a serious medical emergency with an eleven-pound hematoma, fibroid, and tumor in my uterus that was about to birth itself. Considering the many life-threatening situations throughout my life, the years of suicidal ideations, and the ongoing thoughts about death and dying which I survived, this medical situation was just not as frightening to me. I was in a place where I was leaning heavily on God, and I surrendered to whatever the outcome would be. I had somehow overcome my sense of a shortened future, and I welcomed the opportunity to let go of some my body memories and the chronic medical issues, which were caused by my previous childhood sexual abuse.

My main concern was not so much the surgery but rather the anesthesia. I suspected what would happen to me because of

23

traumatic experiences in my past and what it would do to those around me if I didn't speak up, so I asked my surgeon if I could get my anesthesia in pre-op, preferably. I knew very well what alarms would be set off if I was rolled down the hall into the OR if I was not sedated. I knew I would not visibly freak out and could likely manage on the outside, while I was conscious, but I also knew too well that there were no guarantees what would happen after that. Usually, I was in full fight-or-flight mode, trying to literally fight my way out, at all costs, as soon as my system began to wake. It is really embarrassing to wake up to knowing that I was combative and that I could have hurt someone. I always apologized profusely, and after a while people usually calmed down because they could tell that I was getting myself into a better place as I returned to consciousness.

Thanks to my surgeon's initiative in 2009, she met me in pre-op and spent just a little bit of time with me. She had already arranged for the anesthesiologist to meet me in pre-op as well. He came and spoke to me for a moment and while we were talking, he administered the drug. As a result, I not only went to sleep peacefully, but I also woke up as calm as a lamb.

Unfortunately, the follow-up surgery two years later, did not go as well. Though I had the same surgeon, I had a different anesthesiologist whom I saw barely long enough to state my name and birthdate and confirm what type of surgery would be performed on me. It was clear that she was not at all interested in listening to my concerns about triggers that would lead to me panicking because of my trauma history. Instead, she argued that since my heart rate was at forty-five beats per minute in pre-op, I could not possibly experience any form of anxiety. One more time I tried to assert myself and inform her that I would likely decompensate, if I was not sedated before going into the operating room. She quickly dismissed my concerns and hustled out of the room. I tried to be as calm as I could, but when I felt the undoing of the brakes on my hospital bed to be rolled down the long hallway into the OR, and when I observed a male nurse holding up one instrument at a time in preparation for my surgery, I inevitably went down memory lane.

By the time I scooted myself onto the cold operating table, in my mind I was in complete panic mode. All I could do was try not to jump off the table. A large part of me was already wanting to run. My internal self-care system was automatically applying my good old survival mechanisms—namely to completely dissociate.

When I woke up, it took me a moment to realize that I was combative and that the staff was fighting with me, trying to restrain me for my safety as well as for their own. Again, I had to relive being stared at by some innocent helper, who had to fight yet another "crazy patient," who physically attacked them while they were just trying to assist post-surgery. As soon as I regained some level of consciousness, I was able to calm the storm on the inside enough to regain my composure, but as usual, the damage was already done. The sad part is, these experiences are avoidable if people are willing to listen and pay attention to us. When I told my surgeon about what had happened during my second surgery when we had our follow up, she just covered her face and with tears in her eyes profusely apologized. I love her for saving my life, I love and appreciate her even more for respecting me as a human being and for truly listening to me.

REFLECTIONS

Let me explain the issues this completely avoidable experience brought back to me. My worst memory about going into my first-ever surgery dates all the way back to when I was perhaps nine or ten years old. I vaguely remember being dropped off at the hospital for my tonsil surgery by a dissociative parent, who had apparently arranged for the medical procedure but was so detached that she could not render any comfort or emotional support. There was neither any explanation as to what to expect from the medical procedure nor was there anybody who cared enough to stay at the hospital and be there when I woke up from the anesthesia. I remember working myself into complete hysteria, because looking back, I believe I was expecting something terrible to happen to me. I usually didn't allow myself to show strong emotions because I knew better. Yet, my body remembered the physical sensation when the nurses finally came to get me, undid the brakes on my bed, and pushed me into the operating room. By then I was in complete fight-or-flight mode, and I vividly remember being pushed down by several adults onto the operating table, while a nun struggled to drop ether on the mask she was pressing over my mouth. My body remembered that something very similar had already happened to me on a number of occasions, but this was the first time it was done to me in a medical setting. I believe that I was completely hysterical and put up the biggest fight because I was convinced that I was going to die.

To me this is not just an example of poor parenting, but there were much more serious concerns tied into this. Now, looking back, I can imagine that there were some real fears on the part of the abusers, because what if I were to talk or spill the beans so to speak, while under anesthesia. Or what if the medical personnel would discover the marks or bruises all over my body, and what if they would have been found out. By then, I had already been brainwashed and made to believe that I was a bad person, deserved everything that was happening to me, and that nobody cared to listen to what I had to say; therefore, I did not say a word. During that time in my life, some serious traumatic events were happening frequently, and most of the time I had been drugged for the purpose of being abused. When I came to, not only had I lost chunks of time, but I would also be in bad shape, emotionally and physically. Occasionally, I would be rushed to some doctor I had never seen before and who I would never see again. It makes sense to me that I had such a traumatic reaction as a child and that this memory resurfaces to this day, especially when I am not completely conscious.

I wonder if the anesthesiologist for my surgery in 2012 would have felt differently had she known this part of my story, but I honestly doubt that she could have mustered up an ounce of compassion, because she had already turned a deaf ear to my basic request to be treated as a human being. I can only reiterate that we have honestly been through enough, and it is not only unnecessary, but causes additional damage if we are not being heard or if we are being utterly dismissed.

I am sharing this memory with you because I know that I am not the only one who had experiences like these and who gets triggered in some way or another while undergoing some sort of medical procedure. I realize that there is no room for long and in-depth conversations, nor is there any room for all sorts of accommodations to suit everybody according to their individual needs, but clearly, it does not take that much to arrange for a compassionate gesture on the part of the medical team.

I was grateful when I was asked to help accommodate a patient who was in need of surgery and needed her service dog to be as close as possible, that I was part of a medical team that was thinking outside the box. We made accommodations to have her service dog accompany her to the OR area and wait for her in the recovery room, which made it possible for her to manage emotionally and be able to safely undergo her surgery. I believe we all need to re-examine our personal as well as societal norms, our understanding of and our responses to any so-to-speak crisis and our willingness to approach unusual situations if we want to be part of significant changes.

I have so often reflected on the fact that if a person takes cover in reaction to a car's backfiring in the street, most of us would assume that individual perhaps has been under gunfire at some time in their life and are less likely to judge that person. If somebody asks for help with low blood sugar and looks rather faint, most of us would rush to get that individual some juice and perhaps we would get medical assistance. If someone who has a physical disability asks for assistance to get up on a gurney for a medical procedure, most of us would make accommodations, because we can see that the person is clearly at a disadvantage and because we believe them.

Why is it then that when trauma survivors ask for assistance to prevent a panic attack or traumatic reaction before or during a medical procedure, we get so easily devalued, shamed, humiliated, or dismissed? Is it because people cannot see our disability, because people cannot relate, because people do not believe that we are telling the truth, or because people feel that they are a better judge of what we do or do not need? Since none of us really know what is going on inside of an individual, I think it is immensely important for all of us to stay open-minded and compassionate and postpone judgment in any situation, because some of these negative events can truly set off some internal alarms, which could result in some type of self-harm—or worse, in a potential suicide. I have listened to many stories where patients reported that they had been through such severe trauma for years on end, but what eventually made them reach such a drastic measure was that last incident—literally the straw on the camel's back. This expression never really made sense to me because it was too abstract, until I experienced it first hand. After carrying such a heavy load for so long, it was a relatively small event that had my legs go out from underneath me and made me land flat on my face.

I am sharing these intimate experiences in an attempt to provide further insight into what it means to have dealt with complex trauma and how it affects us in the long run, even after going through years of therapy. Though many of us are highly educated and accomplished, and we may have done years of serious work, we are still not completely free from the burden of our adverse experiences. We can still find ourselves in a place of disadvantage and vulnerability, often in the most inopportune times, when our complex trauma gets triggered and we end up reacting in a way that we ourselves are not even prepared for..

I share my own experiences and lived experiences of other survivors, to highlight some of the distinct characteristics of our recovery, and for all of us to be gentle, to postpone judgment, and to let the experiences speak for themselves. To me these experiences are sacred, and they are only being shared for the benefit of other survivors, for the benefit of those who continue to support us, and for those we come into contact with inadvertently. We are neither asking for pity nor do we give permission for those experiences to be distorted or otherwise abused. The goal is to help educate and deepen the understanding for everybody involved and perhaps facilitate a way to avoid unnecessary retraumatization.

CHAPTER 3

ON THE TOPIC OF SUICIDE

I USED PERSONAL EXPERIENCES AS MY starting point, not because I want to trouble the reader with autobiographical facticities, but because I want to draw the reader into the structure and essence of the phenomenon, meaning the nature of complex trauma and its long-term consequences. I share these experiences not because I think they are unique, but because I know that they are universal in nature, meaning they are the experiences of countless other individuals. My intention is to create a platform on which we can have a more open and gentle dialogue about complex trauma and its long-term effects and hopefully, create a space for more understanding and compassion overall. Sadly enough, for those of us who have experienced Adverse Childhood Ecperiences (ACEs), our long-term effects include severe depression and anxiety, sustained fight-or-flight mode, struggles with addiction, overall complicated lives, and dealing with passive or active suicidal ideations.

As you may imagine, for children who are completely powerless in their ongoing toxic situation, death does not seem as horrible as non-survivors might think. Instead, suicide is a backdoor of sorts—a means to exit an incomprehensible situation and seemingly, the only thinkable way out. When we survivors begin healing and quite literally begin putting our fragmented pieces back together, we must inevitably deal with the topic of suicide. For years, we have had to re-evaluate our life situation at every juncture, so when we finally come to a place in our healing where we actually feel that life might be worth living, suicidality as a coping mechanism will not just disappear. In fact, most of us will have to negotiate with our Internal Self-Care system and work toward solutions to life's problems other than the old familiar plan, meaning self-harm, which might include at some point terminating our own life.

Because this way of thinking is often so foreign to non-survivors, my goal is to provide more education about how difficult it is to deal with complex trauma and with its long-term consequences to our friends and family members, our support systems, and our well-meaning allies. I want to illuminate the fact that our adverse childhood experiences often lead to long-term effects well into our adult life, and what we experience is not our choice. It is simply the nature of having lived with ACEs.

It is my hope that the difficult journeys of the individuals I am sharing with the reader will be honored and acknowledged for their incredible battles. Furthermore, I want to reach some of the survivors who struggle with their complex trauma and are fighting to stay alive, so they might feel encouraged to reach out for help before they get to a place where they feel that the only way to end their pain is by taking their lives. I am also trying to demystify some of these difficult topics and help non-survivors have better insight and understanding, so that when survivors reach out, they will be received in a way that lets them know that they are being heard, believed, and at least somewhat understood.

I have chosen a few encounters in connection with suicide attempts I dealt with professionally that will stay with me for as long as I live, because they shed such light on the uniqueness of human experiences as well as their similarities. A few years ago, I met two middle-aged women who happened to find themselves in the same hospital at the same time, and both ended up in the same process group where they eventually became friends. Each learned what had brought them to the emergency services in the first place once they woke up in the hospital. Both had suffered serious self-inflicted injuries during their suicide attempts, and both reported having absolutely no recollection of their actual suicide attempt. While both women were dealing with serious life stressors, neither one recalled having any conscious suicidal thoughts prior to their suicide attempt. Imagine such a complete blackout, and part of the psyche pushing to the forefront, deciding to take such drastic measures because the emotional pain for the individual seemed too overwhelming to continue living.

I would argue that waking up to such a tragic event is probably just as traumatic as it is for any family member or friend to have to deal with the terrible news that a loved one has made a serious suicide attempt. Actually, both women did not have to deal as much with the shame and guilt usually surrounding a suicide attempt and the pain experienced by their loved ones as a result of it. Both women were rather terrified by their own experience and the fact that they had no conscious memory of planning and or carrying out the attempt—and both of them very much wanted to be alive.

Another young woman attempted suicide after learning that the sexual abuse she had experienced, and had overshadowed her adolescent and adult life, had not stopped with her. Two young girls in her family had become the next generation's targets, and had felt comfortable enough to confide in her; they shared with her details about the sexual trauma being inflicted upon them by the same abuser. She explicitly stated she had felt something break inside, and she recalled that after she received the news, she found herself immediately on "autopilot." She was still somewhat functional in ways, but she had become otherwise very much dissociative, during which her suicide attempt occurred. She recalled that by the time she received emergency medical care, she had already become more present and felt extremely remorseful—and she was very grateful to still be alive. She quickly realized that the two pre-teens who had been sexually abused could have lost their number one supporter, and they would have been left without that guardian or advocate they so desperately needed.

Subsequent to her suicide attempt, she became more determined than ever to support the girls on all fronts, even if that meant diving into her own recovery from childhood sexual abuse. She did not want these young girls' present experience with the same abuser to be overshadowed by her own history of abuse and her long-term suffering, because she wanted to be present and emotionally available to them. By the way it is not uncommon, that sexual abuse survivors who were either not heard, not believed, or silenced when they were trying to report their own sexual abuse to their caretakers, become actively involved when they learn of sexual abuse of younger siblings or of sexual abuse of the next generation.

In this case, the abuser was arrested and subsequently brought to trial. Unsurprisingly, the events leading up to the trial triggered painful memories for her, but she managed to separate her feelings to be a support for the young girls. In the end they saw the abuser put behind bars. The experience, however difficult, was very healing for her as an adult survivor of sexual abuse, who was able to protect the next generation from the abuser from whom she had no protection when she was a child. Unfortunately, in her case, the adults in charge of her care were neither as informed nor strong enough to stand up to the patriarch of the family. She felt that because of her own therapy, she was able to support them. These young girls were able to develop their own voices, were able to speak up, and fortunately were being heard in a court of law, unlike so many other sexual-abuse survivors.

A few years back, while I was working at a hospital, I met a young woman post-suicide attempt. I heard about her while she was still unconscious, and I knew that her medical team was fighting to keep her alive. Her attempt alone left absolutely no doubt that she wanted to die, and I could not help but wonder how she'd feel when she woke and if our team would be able to help lift her out of her deep depression and her feelings of despair. When she finally became conscious, she was deeply disappointed that her attempt failed and that she was still here on this earth.

She felt as if, because of her devastating childhood sexual abuse and its long-term consequences, she neither deserved to be alive nor to be the mother to her growing children. In her mind, she felt she was simply not good enough. She was a kind and gentle soul, but none of the interventions seemed to ease her deep despair, which arose from her adverse childhood experiences and continued to torture her every day of her adult life. After she returned home, her family unfortunately lost her shortly after due to her final suicide attempt, which was extremely sad and sobering for everybody involved. I can honestly say this young woman is very much part of my motivation to write this book.

I also met with a number of elderly people who attempted suicide, and it wasn't unusual for them to share with me that, aside from feeling lonely and a lack of purpose, they were exhausted from having to carry the life-long burden of childhood abuse, often sexual in nature. These elderly patients spent their lives attempting to repress their painful memories, yet all reported that their childhood abuse not only overshadowed their entire adult life, but that the pain of these experiences was becoming exceedingly acute well into their later life. A few shared with me that the death of a sibling, who'd likewise been abused but had never disclosed their pain to anyone, left them with significant guilt. Oftentimes, the surviving siblings were left with tremendous pain because they were unable to protect their brother or sister from their abusers while they were all growing up. Usually, those left behind felt a deep desire to reunite with their deceased siblings, as they imagined life after death being a relief from the life-long pain and ugliness of their childhood abuse.

Lastly, I would like to share a narrative I came across in Donald Kalshed's *The Inner World of Trauma*, just a few years ago. Kalshed retells the story of a woman who planned to kill herself when she was only four years old, because she had such a torturous upbringing. One night she went to bed and contemplated running into traffic the next morning. That night she dreamed of an encounter with a fairy. The fairy made it crystal clear to the little girl that death meant the end of absolutely everything, and there'd be no way of going back. The dream had such an impact on her that she changed her plans, and instead of attempting suicide, she created a nurturing fantasy world into which she could escape. On rare occasions, she would be pulled out of her fantasy world into her everyday life. She would become outwardly angry and resentful and displace her anger onto the family dog. As you may imagine, living

33

in such different realities was not only confusing but also extremely painful for the little girl. It was not until she entered her analysis that she could work through the many complex layers of her trauma. I realized that I could very much relate to her, but could not immediately make a conscious connection to my traumatic events and how I personally managed to stay alive. The details of how I survived those suicidal urges in my childhood emerged much later—in fact, they emerged while writing this text.

REFLECTIONS

Because of my experience with people across all social, cultural, and racial lines who've attempted suicide, as well as complex trauma survivors who were struggling with active and/or passive suicidal ideations, I have concluded that their attempts to end their lives are anything but selfish. Most of them felt they were a tremendous burden for everybody around them and they were convinced that their families' lives would be much easier in their absence. I often felt the need to "normalize suicidality," with these patients, reassuring them that any other human being under the same set of circumstances and with identical emotional tool sets would likely feel similar despair, culminating in an attempt to end their lives.

I am grateful I was advanced enough into my own recovery, especially while I was working on the frontline, that I could be transparent with my patients, and share with them that life after recovery is in fact worth living. I wanted them to know that there was hope, and I was able to express to them that I was truly grateful that they were still alive. Most of them could tell I was speaking from personal experience, that I had done my own healing work, and that I was coming from a place of loving kindness, compassion, and a place of knowing. I truly understood how hard their journey really was. The opportunity to connect with patients who attempted suicide has afforded me the ability to make connections, share resources, and co-create safety plans in the event of future circumstances that may catalyze yet another episode of either passive or active suicidality.

I have been trying to share just enough lived experience to show some of the unique dynamics of complex trauma with its long-term consequences as well as the universal response patterns to these devastating early childhood experiences, hoping it will be helpful to survivors and non-survivors alike. Because some individuals, when confronted with details of our extensive trauma, can easily feel overwhelmed, helpless, or unequipped, I am focusing more on the emotional responses than the gory details of our abuse. My goal for the reader is understanding that the trauma we experienced during our formative years, unfortunately, left a deep imprint on our bodies, minds, and souls.

Unfortunately, the cultural stereotypes around survivors of ACEs are such that many of us, though we managed to survive, have difficulty thriving because we are so often met with such a lack of understanding and support by those around us, including some medical teams and even some mental-health professionals. It is crucial to educate survivors and their allies that ongoing and severe levels of anxiety and depression are typical for individuals with four or more ACEs, and that sometimes it is a literal struggle to stay alive.

Fortunately, though, much of the damage can be undone in treatment and with help of sustained loving kindness and compassion from our families, friends, and our larger community—especially the medical community. Those attitudes are paramount to approaching survivors of ACEs because surviving sustained childhood abuse, and the subsequent emotional and social fallout, are not based on our choices. Since we neither asked for nor volunteered to be neglected or maltreated, many of us continually question "why" or "how" we became the targets of such intense, prolonged abuse. Similarly, we spend most of our adult lives questioning our own behaviors that arise from our ACEs, including a vast variety of triggers, severe levels of anxiety accompanied by panic attacks, and, of course, severe levels of depression. In fact, many of us become defined by our ACEs and our seemingly bizarre reactions, which cannot and will not be resolved or undone in a vacuum or without outside help.

35

I shared with you the narrative about the little four-year-old girl who wanted to run into traffic because I felt that her experience so aptly describes a child's perspective when struggling with ongoing abuse. Her story triggered my memory of my own childhood suicidal ideations following my parents' divorce while I was still in elementary school. I conceived of two locations to end my life. One was the busy intersection I crossed daily to get to school where enormous double-decker buses sped through the traffic signal, and the other one was a nearby bridge that spanned over many railroad tracks.

I believe the pure fear of potentially surviving kept me from stepping in front of a speeding bus or from leaping off the overpass in front of a moving train. The reason I was in such deep despair so early in my life was that my homelife included screaming, yelling, cussing, humiliation, and embarrassment, plus gradually increasing physical, emotional, and eventually sexual abuse. There was no love—I knew I was not important—and the people around me were either too drunk or too depressed to take care of me.

The worst punishment for me was by far the deafening silence in our home when the adults stopped conversing with each other for weeks on end and I, by default, became the person in between who had to relate messages or serve the meals that had been prepared. Eventually, I did something wrong and would become part of the bizarre cycle, meaning no one would speak to me either. When the creepy silence went on and on, all I had was a tiny teddy bear, small enough to fit into any of my pockets, who had become my imaginary friend and protector. Unlike the adults in the home, I could confide in or talk to my teddy bear, whenever I needed to. Occasionally, my mother would break her silence but instead of talking to me, she would speak to my teddy bear directly, and relay an important message to me that way.

It just so happened that one day, the little teddy bear fell out of my pocket, completely unnoticed. When I checked my pockets, just before entering the "war zone" that was my home, I noticed that I had lost my little companion. In complete panic I retraced my steps, only to find him lying on the side of the road, completely flattened and dismembered, clearly run over by one of the yellow double-decker buses, which I had likewise hoped would run me over one day. I quickly gathered the pieces of the flattened and dismembered teddy bear and dashed back to the apartment-warzone in hopes an adult could triage my little companion and bring him back to life. To me it was a matter of life and death for my pocket-size teddy bear.

Even as a child, I found it surprising that my mother showed more empathy to my little teddy bear than she had ever shown to me. While I watched her perform emergency surgery, she seemed as genuinely traumatized by his tearing apart as I was. Though she put my little bear back together as best as she could, the only one who I felt I could trust, who loved me, and who cared about me in this life—was never the same. I felt horrible because I had brought this innocent little teddy bear into my life, and I literally felt it was my fault that he got hurt and suffered as much as I did. After the traumatic incident, I dealt with the serious loss I had experienced. I detached myself from everyday life even more by adding another layer of protection, and for a little while, I gave up on the idea of hurting myself because I was dealing with the guilt of hurting someone else.

My mostly passive suicidality stayed with me all throughout my post-traumatic life, as it does for so many other survivors. But as I got older, it took on different forms, and as an adult I realized that I had to consider many other variables and details when it came to suicide. Because of the guilt I felt for hurting my teddy bear as a child, I was not going to consider ending my own life in any manner where I would hurt someone else. It may sound strange, but for long stretches in my life, my suicidal ideations were perhaps my only comfort. For me, mortality was not as scary as someone might think, but it provided a strange sense of relief, because being in the midst of my torture and abuse, at least I knew there would be some end in sight, eventually.

It took decades to begin my own healing journey and examine the long-term consequences of my early abuse, which had such negative effects on absolutely every aspect of my life. In the process of my journey, it eventually allowed me to understand not only what happened to me but what happened inside of me. I slowly learned how to stop judging myself so harshly and how to slowly reduce my negative self-talk I had grown accustomed to. I was able to develop some compassion for myself, began to understand my ineffectual coping mechanisms, and I acquired an awareness of my tactical defense mechanisms that no longer served me. Finally, I developed a sense of hope for the future, let go of my passive thoughts of suicide, and for the first time in my life, I felt that I was ready and able to embrace life and everything that comes with it.

One of the most difficult aspects for us as trauma survivors is that we feel badly about ourselves, and our default leads to feeling completely undeserving and defective, often resulting in either diminishing or harming ourselves, which is very difficult to live with. Eventually, on our healing journey, we learn to better manage our lives, which results in inner peace and a sense of gratitude for our resiliency and inner strength. It might explain, though, to the reader, why we can have strong reactions when we have to deal with avoidable retraumatization, when we are met with the same toxic and negative treatment we have experienced all along and worked so hard to get away from.

See, societies as well as individuals are usually reluctant to face their own objectionable behavior and are, therefore, prone to minimization and denial. Unfortunately, the truth is that there are vast numbers of children in our society today that are being mildly, moderately, and severely harmed, resulting from abuse and neglect in their home. Paradoxically, the lack of recognition and denial of its prevalence not only causes turmoil and controversy, but also has tremendous implications on our sociological and even political perspectives and behaviors. As a society, it is paramount to not only recognize the prevalence of adverse childhood experiences, but also acknowledge the long-term impact it has on adult survivors who invariably suffer from their complex trauma, which cannot only be extremely debilitating but also potentially continue the vicious cycle for generations to come.

38

The latter begs the question, what are we willing to do for those who are dealing with the long-term consequences of their abuse, and how will we support them on their incredibly difficult journeys? Because to silence us in a court of law, to dismiss our specific needs during a medical procedure, or to discredit our trauma reactions to something that causes us to relive our original trauma not only re-traumatised us, but also feeds into the shame, guilt, and defeat loop we have lived in for a lot longer than you might imagine. To dismiss us, to misunderstand and misinterpret our specific needs, and to accuse us of things we have not done, especially when we turn to law enforcement or the judicial system for support and protection, is tantamount to our original trauma.

The fallout after we survivors have been treated so poorly is very significant and simply feeds into the same cycle of abuse, creates the same negativity and hopelessness, and leads to feelings of shame and guilt. Therefore, the inability and unwillingness to recognize a trauma survivor's special needs appropriately and accurately is a serious societal failure, especially by professionals within the medical system, law enforcement, and the judicial system, who should clearly be better equipped to support us.

Please remember, most of us have been brainwashed by our perpetrators for many years and been accused of things we never did. We have been told over and over that we deserved our abuse, that our pain is not real, and if we told anybody even part of our story, nobody would believe us anyway. Most of those messages were given to us at an early age, and we had no way of knowing any differently because we were so young. These messages became part of our fabric of life, and it has taken many of us a long, *long* time and a lot of inner work to try to undo this type of thinking.

It is honestly painful when we turn to medical teams, law enforcement, or any judicial branch after we have been involved in a major accident, we are truly in need of a medical intervention, we have been sexually assaulted, or whatever it may be, and we are being dismissed, belittled, or tossed aside only because we have a traumatic past. Being denied the most fundamental component of our lives today, which is to be able to feel safe, heard, understood, and met with some level of compassion, can be extremely difficult for complex trauma survivors.

Depending on the severity of our abuse, depending where we are in our recovery, and depending on the level of indignity we are being met with, these avoidable traumatic experiences, can unfortunately be likened to a second rape, because any type of violation, alienation, and disparagement is certainly not what a survivor needs or deserves when he or she turns to others for help. As a society at large we need to make significant changes, so that the betrayal complex trauma survivors have already experienced within the original trauma, will no longer be continued or perpetuated.

PART 2

CHAPTER 4

THE DIFFERENT FACES OF TRAUMA

ONE DEFINITION OF *TRAUMA* IS that it "consists of an exceedingly difficult or unpleasant experience, which causes someone to have mental or emotional problems usually for a long time" (Miriam Webster). The word *trauma* comes from the Greek word for *wound*, a term freely used for "either physical injuries caused by a direct external force or for psychological injury caused by an extreme emotional assault" (*The Penguin Dictionary of Psychology*). Pervasive trauma or complex trauma, describes repetitive abuse and/or profound neglect which usually takes place early in a child's life and is often perpetrated by some type of caregiver, which means it disrupts many aspects of a child's development and interferes especially with the formation of a sense of self and with the formation of secure attachments (National Child's Traumatic Stress Network, NCTSN). These multiple traumatic experiences are often of invasive and of interpersonal nature, which explains why they have such wide-ranging, long-term effects.

Causes for trauma are, in general, events such as accidents, physical and sexual assaults, or natural disasters, and reactions to trauma are usually described as deeply overwhelming, distressing, dangerous, or disturbing events which exceed one's ability to cope and the traumatic experiences may elicit emotional responses that leave the person in shock, disbelief, or with feelings of pure terror. The reactions can range anywhere from fear to a fight, flight, or freeze reaction, and might leave the individual with symptoms such as hyper vigilance, flashbacks, complete numbness, as well as denial.

Levels of psychological trauma are generally placed into three categories. Acute trauma is caused by single traumatic events such as an accident, rape, or natural disaster. Chronic trauma is caused by multiple traumatic events, exemplified by either multiple natural disasters, war, refugee situations, domestic violence, or human trafficking. And complex trauma, which is a result of poly victimization, like chronic trauma, but in addition we have to consider other serious aspects, such as a deep sense of betrayal, because the traumatic events were human-made, and because they seriously interfered with the natural developmental stages of the child or adolescent. Therefore, complex trauma has longer lasting effects deep into adulthood, compared to the effects of trauma that was not perpetrated by another human being and does not include the component of betrayal.

Consequences of trauma include the loss of trust in humanity, a fear of vulnerability, a fear of showing emotions and with that the need to avoid anger and sadness, as well as a phobia for any type of dependency. As complex trauma survivors, most of us were severely punished for expressing any type of emotion (Janine Fisher, *Transforming the Living Legacy of Trauma*). We knew our caretakers could not be trusted, and we experienced over and over the exploitation of our physical and emotional needs. Therefore, our radar for any type of betrayal, any type of pretense, any type of lie, and any hidden danger is often larger than life, which should come as no surprise. With that being said, it may make sense that we feel the need to pay attention to pretty much everything, we need safeties that non-survivors have a difficult time relating to, and it often takes us a long time before we allow ourselves to trust anybody close to us.

The destruction of the integrity of the soul and annihilation of that which makes us human has been given the name *soul murder* for over a century. Wirtz speaks of having experienced *hell* and of *liminality* in her work, the psychological process of moving across the threshold, the space in between consciousness and unconsciousness, between life and death. In trauma therapy, we can observe that as a rule the encounter with *evil* elicits one of four typical responses: fight, flight, freeze, and fragmentation. Trauma work consists of bringing the estranged parts of psyche/soul home and moving from fragmentation to integration. This means severe-trauma survivors need assistance with bringing their broken-off aspects back into the whole, with the ability to get into contact with the *Thou*, the presence of the uniqueness and wholeness in and of another person, and with returning the flow back to their own stream of life (Wirtz, 2014).

> In the spiritual borderland of traumatic loss of meaning, in the black hole of despair and hopelessness, human beings feel no longer in relationship with the totality of being, but alone, having fallen out of all familiar, meaning-creating connections. This frightening, unfamiliar, numinous dimension into which their (traumatic) experiences have thrown them produces a far-reaching estrangement from (their) ego and the world. Traumatized individuals have become lost to themselves and to their environment, helplessly (existing) at the mercy of a silent cosmos (Wirtz, 2014).

As a wounded healer myself, I feel rather familiar with the landscape of liminality and working in the borderland between traumatic loss of meaning and the black hole of hopelessness and despair. In fact, I often use mythology working with complex trauma survivors in therapy, and I liken our work to a mutual journey to and from the underworld. I know from experience that as a survivor it is extremely helpful to have somewhat of a roadmap, and it is extremely helpful to know that the professional we are working with has a good understanding of what it means to undertake a journey of death and rebirth. Dealing with our shadow aspects head on, meaning those aspects about ourselves none of us wish to face, is rather difficult and challenging work, but it is also very necessary if we truly want to get to our authentic self.

Some of the most important lessons I learned from mythology are, one, we need a loyal companion who will shift into action when

45

we do not return and are missing in action; two, not to go into the underworld unprepared, but to have a backup plan that can be followed when things get more dire than expected; and three, understand how to plead with the gods for the super-natural support we may need, because we may not be able to return if we were left to our own devices. And finally, the amazing payoff for undertaking such a risky journey, is the transformation of no longer having to live in the world of extremes, of either black or white, but the fact that the journey gradually enables us to live in both worlds, the dark as well as the light, simultaneously.

My goal is to lay the foundation for the reader to be more prepared to deal with and have a better understanding of the dynamics underlying complex trauma. Together, we will explore the different faces of trauma, the stages of trauma recovery, and the long-term consequences of childhood maltreatment. We will look at the traumatic brain and traumatic memory, as well addiction, dissociation, and how our internal self-care system might step in when survivors are triggered. Finally, we will explore the purpose of this phenomenological inquiry, the need for compassion, and how survivors and non-survivors can better support each other.

The reason for the discussion of these selected topics is, as you will see, that the changes we underwent during our developmental years were so significant they caused our brain to be on alert 24/7, we continue scanning our surroundings for any type of threat, and we keep reacting according to what is familiar to us. We will simply continue to interpret our life events according to our negative experiences until we find the right help and are able to slowly make the necessary adjustments, meaning we eventually get to rewire our brain. It would be great if time really healed all wounds, but that is unfortunately not so, especially for complex trauma survivors, for the many reasons we will be able to explore together. Because our healing journey takes a lot of effort, patience, courage, and resources, it may make sense that increased levels of compassion, understanding, and support on the part of all involved will definitely better enable us to make these significant changes which will improve the quality of our lives, and the lives of those around us, drastically.

CHAPTER 5

THE STAGES OF RECOVERY

GENERALLY, TRAUMA RECOVERY IS THOUGHT of as survivors being able to live in the present, no longer haunted by old memories, but that is not all of what trauma recovery is about. As much as survivors are longing for healing, and as much as our family members and friends wish for us to be able to recover, it is important to remember that trauma recovery is a very individual experience, which not only takes a lot of time, strength, willpower, and patience, but is also a unique and different journey for everybody going through the process. The truth is that we find freedom by working through our trauma, gathering new evidence that life can be worth living, and that not every negative experience will turn into a life-or-death matter. But as complex trauma survivors, we also need to develop new coping mechanisms and brand-new problem-solving skills, which we have never used before. In the process, we have to deal with this thing called *middle ground*, for which we have absolutely no reference. In our black-and-white world it has always been *all or nothing*—for as long as we have lived. Eventually, our past negative experiences will gradually be less and less capable of haunting us in the way they did for way too long. While we do not forget what happened to us, we eventually get a chance to learn about who we really are, and we develop tools that enable us to let go and move forward, so that our trauma history no longer dictates our post-trauma lives.

47

In the early 2000s, I came across Judith Herman's book, *Trauma and Recovery*, while I was finishing up my PhD, and I have to say that it had a huge impact on me personally and professionally. Things finally began making sense to me, as far as what to focus on in the treatment of trauma and why our recovery takes more time and is a bit more challenging than the recovery from some neurotic issues. Just reading the text helped me realize all the different issues I had been trying to work through. Though I was not privileged to work with a trained trauma therapist, this provided helpful steps in my trauma recovery. I no longer felt so alone and awkward because of what I had experienced and the way I had been trying to maneuver through my post-trauma life for so many years.

It made so much sense to me that trauma recovery would first focus on establishing internal and external safety and stability, developing inner strengths and additional inner resources, regulating emotions, avoiding overwhelm, and developing skills to minimize unhelpful responses. Second, it focuses on remembrance and mourning, which includes reviewing and processing painful memories to reduce their intensity, working through grief regarding unwanted and traumatic experiences, revising one's own meaning of life and one's sense of identity, and mourning the loss of a healthy upbringing with all its opportunities for healthy growth and development. And third, it focuses on reconnection with people, creating meaningful activities, and learning to focus on the positive aspects of our everyday life (Herman, 1997).

Again, we need to remember that just like the stages of grief can show up so differently for different people and may show up in any order, so do the stages of recovery for the individual trauma survivor. Most of us are struggling with painful memories, mourning the loss of our childhood or teenage years, engulfed in struggles with some type of addiction, and feel overwhelmed and stuck in our post-trauma life. So, when we eventually find our way into therapy, it makes sense that the main focus needs to be on our safety, stability, and developing inner strength and resources, so that we can safely enter the next phase of trauma recovery, where we are dealing with all of our painful memories. What we survivors generally have in common before therapy is the fact that we find ourselves all over the map because we have been living in a different universe. We usually have not had any type of road map for our unusual journey, and I believe I speak for many of us when I say that re-entering Planet Earth is a difficult task. In that phase, informed and compassionate support is helpful.

At about the same time I learned about the stages of recovery, I also learned in my graduate classes that there is something called the *human experience*, which to me meant I was truly not the only one feeling the way I felt or the only one acting the way I had acted—others may have had similar life experiences. It was a bit of a shock at first, which slowly turned into relief, and then it became comforting for me to realize that human beings under similar pressures and circumstances use similar defenses. As I studied some of Carl G. Jung's work, I began appreciating that those of us who grew up without any opportunity to develop a level of wholeness—but instead had to fragment early on into separate, autonomous, and conflicting parts—continuously fight for wholeness and inner peace. In fact, Jung stated that it is a universal human desire and dream to become whole and have inner peace, and that we are all striving for something similar, which made me feel a lot less isolated and alone.

It made even more sense to me that Jung's work with trauma survivors not only focused on restoring his patient's sense of wholeness, but it also focused on strengthening his patient's psyche, so they could withstand any "future dismemberment." To me, it so adequately puts words on the difficult post-trauma experiences we survivors often encounter, which I had not been able to express on my own. It not only validated my own sense of dismemberment during my upbringing, but it also validated the fact that the many unnecessary negative and retraumatizing experiences even long after our original trauma subsided, can so easily intensify our lingering long-term effects. They not only made me feel dismembered again, but they often caused a serious setback, catapulting me back into my own familiar universe.

Looking back, I realized that not having any therapy for two decades after my original trauma, like so many other complex trauma survivors, I was completely unprepared for my post-trauma life—especially for the long-term consequences leading to unnecessarily retraumatizing experiences, which I had known nothing about. Gaining this insight and understanding at that point in my life made me feel compelled, initially, to give voice to our complicated journey and plead for more trauma-informed and compassionate care and support in our everyday lives. I was very aware that I still had to grow and develop before I could adequately and compassionately communicate what I was and still am so passionate about.

From time to time, I just want to shout ENOUGH has to be ENOUGH. Considering what we have been through, most of us are literally exhausted from our long and serious journey, hoping for a small break so we can have a moment to regroup, reorient, and reset our internal system. Loving kindness and compassion go a very long way for all of us, especially if we find ourselves in a place of vulnerability. I honestly hope that this phenomenological inquiry can help raise some levels of understanding and compassion.

CHAPTER 6

LONG-TERM EFFECTS OF CHILDHOOD MALTREATMENT

LET ME REVIEW WITH YOU the World Health Organization's definition of child maltreatment to highlight what adverse childhood experiences encompass, laying the groundwork for understanding the main long-term consequences we survivors are struggling with. Abuse and/or neglect that occurs to children under eighteen years of age, and includes all types of physical and emotional maltreatment, sexual abuse, neglect, negligence, and commercial or other exploitation that results in actual or potential harm to the child's health, survival, development, or dignity in the context of a relationship of responsibility, trust, or power (The *WHO*).

One of the best resources for this chapter, in my opinion, is the Adverse Childhood Experience Study that was conducted in the 1990s and collaborated among Kaiser Permanente's Health Appraisal Center, the Center for Disease Control and Prevention, and the Emory University in Atlanta, GA. At the time, the US Surgeon General had declared suicide a national priority, because it was and still is one of the leading causes of death among adolescents and young adults. The study ended up highlighting the correlations between adverse childhood experiences and serious health issues, as well as the risk for depression, substance abuse, and suicidality.

The study included adverse childhood experiences such as emotional, physical, and sexual abuse, as well as neglect, household dysfunction, household substance abuse, domestic violence, separation and divorce, household mental illness, and incarceration of a family member, experienced between the ages of 0–18. The ACEs score is rated on a scale from 0–10, with each type of trauma mentioned scoring one point. The findings showed a high correlation between toxic stress growing up and the increase in negative health outcomes for such illnesses as COPD, Hepatitis C, heart and autoimmune disease, and malignancy (CDC-Kaiser, ACE study, 1995 - 1997).

In fact, a score of four or more on the ACEs scale increases the risk for depression four times and the risk for suicidality twelve times. A score of six or more points can simply double or triple the risk for suicidality and or serious health issues. Other long-term effects of toxic stress during childhood development are emotional distress, poor emotional regulation, increased impulsivity, learning disabilities, risk-taking behavior, and other physical and mental health problems. What the study could not account for was the severity and extent of the traumatic experiences, what type of resiliency factors were or were not present in the individual's life, and the fact that individuals respond very differently to traumatic experiences. Therefore, the study can only be used as an indicator to identify individuals who are at a greater risk, but it cannot predict the likelihood for an individual to have a poor outcome later in life or not.

Dr. Vincent Filitti, who was one of the original researchers on the ACEs study, states that one in eleven people in the US score a six or above on the ACEs scale. Considering that a score of six or higher increases the likelihood of becoming an IV drug user and increases the risk for depression and suicide exponentially, these findings rightfully changed much of our medical and mental health communities. Dr. Filitti has observed in his own work as an Internal Medicine doctor, that once patients are able to at least talk about what happened to them as a child, they already experience some level of relief. He makes it a point as a healthcare provider, to ASK questions about difficult subjects, to LISTEN to difficult stories, and to ACCEPT people for their human complexity. He feels that simply acknowledging that ACEs matter in a patient's current overall health can be of great value and can lead to positive changes (Filetti, 2002).

In many cases in psychiatry the patient who comes to us has a story that is not told, and which as a rule no one knows of. To my mind, therapy only begins after the investigation of that wholly personal story. It is the patient's secret, the rock against which he is shattered (Jung, 1963).

The opiate crisis in the United States is one of the biggest crises that claims unbelievable numbers of human life every single year. Dr. Gabor Mate rightfully asks the question why there is not much more public outrage or public alarm, knowing that every three weeks we lose the equivalent of the lives lost on 9/11/2001. If we then consider that ACEs are a main contributor to our opiate crisis, I think we will all have to rethink our priorities and face the fact that the opiate crisis is not an isolated issue. It should be of great concern to all of us.

Dr. Nadine Burke-Harris completely changed her career from being a pediatrician to becoming a researcher, a dedicated physician, and a passionate ACEs advocate after the study's results were published. As the California Surgeon General since 2019, she not only established early childhood health equity, but she also made ACEs and toxic stress her key priorities in her current position. She recently reiterated that she feels ACEs are very likely the number one unaddressed public crisis in our society today, and she reminds us of the importance of reducing the amount of toxic stress on our children. A survivor herself, her goal is to change society's response to this major health crisis and support the efforts to make more education and prevention strategies available than what we currently have (Burke-Harris, 2015).

It is hard to give what your brain has never received. While we now know that trauma survivors can create new neurons, new synaptic connections between those neurons, and new patterns of thoughts and reactions and by doing so, reset our stress responses

53

during our healing journey, one thing we know we will not be able to change, retroactively, is that we have handed down some form of maltreatment to our offspring, inadvertently, and that is a heavy weight to bear (Nakazawa, 2021).

Too many of us were nowhere near being ready to deal with life itself, let alone were ready to be positive parents, no matter how hard we tried. Many ACEs survivors have experienced similar struggles trying to raise children and respond to them appropriately while dealing with post-trauma issues, including severe anxiety, depression, and PTSD symptoms, simultaneously. Many of us tried to be better parents than our own, simply by doing everything opposite what was done to us. While that strategy proved somewhat helpful while our children were small, it often failed horribly when our children grew older, and we were faced with much more complex and emotionally intense issues.

Research studies on the intergenerational effects of childhood maltreatment have revealed some very important insight on the parenting practices of survivors of childhood abuse. Adverse childhood experiences and in particular, poly victimizations have an especially adverse impact on us as children which often extends into our adulthood. There have been many studies on the toll that is inflicted on us as victims and on the risk of intergenerational transmission of maltreatment by us onto the next generation. Growing evidence suggests that childhood maltreatment experiences do affect parenting practices. The newer studies look at the full range of parenting behaviors including abusive parenting, problematic parenting, positive parenting behaviors, and positive parental affect. Some researchers have found that parents who experienced physical abuse during their childhood were more likely to engage in physically aggressive behaviors toward their child. Other studies have shown that it is two to three times more likely for adults who have a child maltreatment history to perpetrate some childhood physical abuse themselves than for those who do not have such a history. There appears to be a cumulative impact of multiple types of victimization or maltreatment of a child, indicating that it is associated with a greater likelihood of perpetrating physical abuse and/or neglect onto one's own children (Greene, Haisley, Wallace, and Ford, 2020).

Looking back, I can clearly see that I was engaging in forms of problematic parenting, including role reversal, inconsistent discipline, permissive parenting, and rejection or withdrawal. For me the inconsistent discipline and the permissive parenting went hand in hand because I wanted to give my children the opportunity to learn to control their own behaviors and make their own choices, because I had never had choices as a child. Due to my untreated and unresolved trauma and my dissociative symptoms, I would not only withdraw for periods of time, but I also resorted to harsh and aggressive treatment when I felt emotionally overwhelmed. With that I was unfortunately, at times, unable to meet my children's needs appropriately.

As a survivor of poly childhood maltreatment who became a parent early in life, I am owning the fact that I was hoping my children would meet my emotional need to be loved, considering they did not know about my awful history and I had completely changed my life around for them. Like many other survivors, it was my deepest desire that my children would never have to grow up like I did. Repeatedly, I was not able to avoid transmitting at least some levels of generational maltreatment to my children and therefore, unfortunately, to my children's children—which is extremely disheartening to me.

Children are a great incentive and impetus for parents to learn about themselves, about each other, and about life itself. Unfortunately, much of our learning occurs at their expense, which Dr. Mate assures us is not a new phenomenon, but has gone on for generations. He encourages those of us who survived severe childhood trauma and ended up ill prepared for parenting children to continue moving forward and not be too dismayed. He encourages us that while the damage itself cannot be undone, the dynamics can eventually be corrected, and according to Dr. Mate, the best way to do that is to work on correcting ourselves, which is not an easy thing to do, especially when we do not understand what is happening to us and where to turn to get the help so desperately needed (Mate, 2012).

It is my hope that some readers will benefit from this discussion, and that they will be encouraged to reach out for help, understanding that their thoughts and behaviors are not as unique and awkward as they think—that they are not *bad people*. But what they are dealing with is a natural consequence of experiencing horrific abuse. There is evidence that healing is possible, and healing is the best thing we can all do for the benefit of our children and our children's children, and in so doing break the generational patterns of abuse.

CHAPTER 7

A BRIEF REVIEW OF THE TRAUMATIC BRAIN

THE THREE AREAS IN OUR brain that are mostly affected by ongoing toxic stress caused by adverse childhood experiences are the amygdala, the hippocampus, and the hypothalamus. Studies have shown those regions of the brain often continue to function in the way they were conditioned to during the ongoing trauma, even when the original trauma subsides. The amygdala, a small bundle of neurons that are almond shaped and located in both sides of our brain and are in charge of detecting and mitigating fear responses, plays a central role in our decision making, emotional responses, and processing of memory. The hippocampus is located close to our primitive brain and is in charge of overcoming fear responses, meaning the regulation of fear and aggression, as well as storing and retrieving memory. It also plays an important role in consolidating short-term to long-term memory into even more enduring permanent memory. It is also in charge of spatial memory, which is necessary for our ability to navigate in space. The most important function of the hypothalamus is to connect our nervous system with our endocrine system, which is made up of the different hormones in our body, by sending signals to the pituitary gland which basically leads to abnormal regulation of cortisol levels, which in turn leads to pathophysiology (Van der Kolk, 2014).

Researchers have discovered within the last decade that the structure, organization, and activity of the brain are negatively affected by adverse childhood experiences, and disruption of the chemical signals, especially during this early period of life which is very much experience-dependent, leads to major abnormalities and deficits in a child's neuro development. This means the developing central nervous system (CNS) is not only sensitive to but also dependent upon environmental input, which has a direct effect on CNS plasticity, or the ability to be shaped, as well as overt behavior. Behavioral plasticity refers to the notion that the child is undergoing a sensitive period where external influences lead to changes in adaptation, learning, memory, and endurance (Weiss, Sheldon & Wagner, 1998).

The amygdala and the hippocampus are seen as the main targets of childhood adversity in a child's brain, and we now know that they are often permanently altered due to childhood trauma, abuse, and maltreatment. Since these brain structures become maladaptive or dysfunctional, and the conditioning of their functionality usually remains into adulthood, it may be less difficult to understand why adult survivors of childhood trauma often have to deal with extreme vulnerabilities, even when they are dealing with seemingly "normal" adult stressors. The goal of the treatment of complex trauma survivors is clearly the mitigation and/or potential reversal of these changes in brain structure and functionality, in order to allow for and facilitate increasing nerve growth in these affected areas. For that to occur, the survivor needs to be in a supportive, non-abusive environment which allows for corrective experiences to occur and for new nerve paths to be shaped (Lamphier, 2021).

One of the main difficulties for survivors of complex trauma is the fact that they do not have a healthy stress response, meaning when they get alarmed by something, they cannot turn off their internal alarm and return to their baseline once they recognize that the danger is over or that their fear response is no longer warranted. Instead they often get stuck in the first half of the stress cycle experiencing hyperarousal and hyper stress reactivity, and they are unable to move into the second half of the cycle. They get stuck in their fight, flight, or freeze responses, perhaps for hours and sometimes even for days.

As we can see, time alone does not heal all wounds, because the survivor's neurological and behavioral maladaptivity and deficits can literally continue to tick away on the inside for decades, like a time bomb, even after the original trauma has stopped. Too often, the impact of the toxic stress levels experienced throughout their childhood continue to dictate their stress reactivity level in their adulthood, and perhaps for the rest of their lives. Studies have shown that important components of a complex trauma survivor's emotional brain actually shrink, due to constantly working overtime, which in turn shrink their ability to process emotions and regulate stress. Furthermore, some of the most recent research has shown that while these toxic stress levels do not necessarily change the DNA, they can change how the DNA is being expressed. These epigenetic differences prevent the brain from being able to appropriately regulate emotional responses, meaning that complex trauma survivors who have dealt with ongoing toxic stress during their childhood development, simply do not have a regular set of "emotional brakes" (Nakazawa, 2021).

While the human brain is designed to tolerate severely stressful situations, it is not designed to deal with milder, prolonged traumatic experiences, especially if they are unpredictable and stretch over a number of early developmental stages. The common denominator for all adverse childhood experiences is their unpredictability and the sense of never knowing what is going to happen next. Therefore, many complex trauma survivor's brains are constantly on hyper alert and hyperarousal. Their brains are basically "marinating" in those inflammatory chemicals, often for decades. Again, the higher the ACEs score the higher the likelihood that all areas in the brain, including the prefrontal cortex, the amygdala, the hippocampus, the hypothalamus, and the cerebellum have been negatively impacted and that their levels of functioning are reduced, which are necessary for decision making, self-regulatory skills, processing fear, and mood regulation (Nakazawa, 2021).

Another major deficiency in complex trauma survivors is the ability to accurately interpret events, which is often a difficult undertaking for them, considering their past experience that they will use as reference for the current event they are dealing with—which generally leads to mostly negative interpretations. Because their emotional life is largely housed in the limbic system, also referred to as the emotional brain, they are likely not able to access other parts of their brain (i.e., the rational part of the brain). Therefore, they have difficulty appraising any present stressful situation, without going into fight, flight, freeze mode, depending on what their default defenses have been in the past.

Those who suffer from complex trauma should be considered as predominantly dealing with a limbic disorder, and they should be treated accordingly. Truth is that recovery from complex trauma takes a tremendous amount of resilience and inner strength, because it is such a challenging and difficult journey. Survivors struggle extremely hard to put their lives into some type of order, especially after losing complete faith in humanity, not being able to trust anybody for the longest time, feeling that the world is not a safe place, and having a sense of a foreshortened future. I feel very strongly that they do not deserve to be treated poorly or to be singled out, because their lives do not fit into any "normal" category. As a matter of fact, I honestly believe most trauma survivors are in many ways stronger and perhaps more resilient than others who did not have to survive the unthinkable atrocities and the traumatic life experiences they had to endure. I truly believe that survivors of complex trauma should be treated with as much compassion, dignity, and respect as anyone else.

Furthermore, the maladaptive behaviors and cognition of complex trauma survivors are not as unique or bizarre as some may want to think. In fact, research has shown that survivors of different kinds of adverse childhood experiences, different levels of maltreatment, and different levels of intensity respond in very similar neurological and behavioral ways. With that in mind though, to expect complex trauma survivors to "just get over it" or "leave the past in the past" or "snap out of things" is something that is clearly impossible to do. Additionally, being met with harsh judgment and ignorance over and over again in adulthood, which invalidates everything they are still experiencing internally, is not only excruciatingly painful but also hinders the recovery process. Dismissing complex trauma survivors' pain and suffering proves to them again and again that the world is not a safe place, nobody cares, and their experiences really do not matter. The lack of compassion and the negative comments they so often encounter are not only uncalled for, but they only add to the already existing pain and suffering, especially if the survivor is being blamed for something he or she did not do or is something they have had absolutely no control over.

As you can see, overcoming the after-effects of adverse childhood experiences is not an easy process and takes time and a lot of effort. While recovery from those after effects is certainly possible, it can neither be forced nor will it take place while the survivor is still dealing with ongoing abuse, or living in a non-supportive environment. Unfortunately, complex trauma survivors are asked over and over again why they are still dealing with the issues of the past. The answer may be as simple as they have not had the opportunity to work on their issues yet, perhaps because they are lacking support or resources, because they are still living in chaos, or because they are still stuck in an abusive situation. Whatever it may be, I know being met with compassion and understanding is one of the most important and powerful experiences they can ever have, and those corrective experiences are extremely helpful in their struggle toward recovery.

CHAPTER 8

A BRIEF REVIEW OF TRAUMATIC MEMORY

MEMORY CAN BE UNDERSTOOD AS the ability or capacity for organization and reconstruction of past experiences. If trauma is defined as an inescapable stressful event that overwhelms people's coping mechanisms, then we have to factor into the equation that traumatic memories are laced with the negative emotional experiences at the time of the traumatic event(s). The uniqueness of traumatic memory is a topic which has been rather controversial for many years, mainly because traumatic memory is very difficult to study. One of the main reasons is there is so little similarity between witnessing traumatic events in a laboratory setting where participants will watch serious traumatic events on a screen, or they are made to believe their decision is causing another person horrendous pain. While the laboratory experiences evoke mechanisms for self-conservation and resource reallocation, they really can not be compared to lived traumatic experiences that have led to the development of complex PTSD over time. Prolonged trauma involves a combination of reactions and responses from hyperarousal, to altered neurological processes, to a shattered sense of self, to learned helplessness and social apprehension. The pathogenic, harmful mechanisms that led to the development of complex PTSD interfered especially with the memory process, and these traumatic memories are usually retrieved via mental imprints of sensory and affective elements of the traumatic experience,

63

making traumatic memories truly unique (Van der Kolk, Hopper, & Osterman, 2002).

When the information about the traumatic event reaches the amygdala, it immediately attaches emotional significance to these events in the process. Sensory stimuli have been transferred into hormonal signals before the prefrontal cortex can consciously appraise the information. Once the amygdala has assigned emotional significance, the information will then be passed on to our hippocampus, which will then organize and categorize the information. The stronger the hippocampus will attend to the information and retain the memory, the higher the levels of emotional stress or arousal the survivor will experience, the more disruption in the process of proper evaluation and categorization. The more emotional significance the amygdala assigns, the more likely it is for the survivors to generate strong emotional responses to any triggers of the traumatic memory, such as anger and/or withdrawal, self-harm and/or suicidal ideations, and any type of acting out, and in some cases these reactions will all be present at once.

The hippocampus, which is an important part of our emotional brain and mainly in charge of learning and memory, is recording all data at lightning speed. Due to chronically high cortisol levels in complex trauma survivors, over time the volume of the hippocampus is reduced, and with that reduction, it will eventually record negative events over positive events. Additionally, the hippocampus will also register the traumatic responses that went along with the traumatic experiences and attach the emotions to the traumatic events. It is not surprising then, that when trauma survivors remember the negative events, they also recall the way they felt at the time the event happened without understanding why, and they might resort to reacting in a similar fashion to the triggering event as they did when the original event occurred.

Children who are exposed to sexual abuse and other severe forms of abuse often use repression or amnesia to cope with their trauma. Representations of the trauma have been encoded in their memory, often in the form of intrusive images, bodily feelings, repetitive dreams, and other mental or behavioral symptoms.

Furthermore, the negative impact of infantile and childhood amnesia on the cognitive, physiological, and environmental changes which normally occur over the course of child development can be seen in areas of trust, autonomy, initiative, industry and identity formation. These representations most often persist long after the original trauma has subsided way into adulthood and affect most subsequent experiences. The unconscious memories may be recovered in response to certain cues in the environment and evoke similar cognitive and behavioral reactions and responses in the survivor, which may even be outside of their control (Kihlstrom, 1995).

Some of the most typical effects of traumatic memories on the survivor are repetition, compulsion, startle responses, over reaction, severe sleep disorders, and recurrent nightmares. Gaps and breaks in the memory of a survivor may simply be a testimony to the disruptive experiences and relate to the reliving of the trauma which often collapses the past into the present. Trauma sometimes assumes the form of unspeakable experiences, endless melancholie, and impossible mourning (LaCapra, 2016).

In an attempt to cope with real and perceived threats, survivors may resort to becoming workaholics and perfectionists, overuse or underuse food, and use and abuse alcohol or other substances to diminish the emotional pain, which can again lead to a number of self-destructive behaviors, including suicidal thoughts and urges to self-harm. These default behaviors may have induced a sense of safety while the survivor experienced the trauma in the past, and they will often be deployed, at least initially, when the survivor is reminded of the original trauma, because these mechanisms are often still in place long after the original trauma subsided.

Understanding these dynamics may explain to survivors as well as their supporters why survivors act at times as if they were back in the past, why they are reliving the toxic experiences, and why they may be reaching to old coping mechanisms, which in turn may create further unsafe situations. Since children are usually less powerful than their abuser, they have to develop defense mechanisms other than fight or flight reactions, as those are not viable options, because of the unfavorable power distribution. So they often resort to some type of freeze response or dissociate, meaning they shut down in one way or another and end up practically paralyzed, and depending on their level of fragmentation, different parts of the self will use different mechanisms at different times.

As a result of the inward retreat, dissociation is often used as the primary defense mechanism. It makes sense that mental contents, especially those attached to traumatic events, are stored in separate compartments of the mind, due to the fragmentation of the self; therefore, memories get connected to and are held by different aspects of the self. One of the main goals on the healing journey from complex PTSD is to learn to accept these traumatic memories and find a way to combine the different aspects of the self into a more integrated and unified self, which often leads to a way for the survivor to finally be able create a more purposeful and peaceful life for themselves.

Many complex trauma survivors have dealt with events that happened while their thinking brain was offline and their primitive brain, also called the reptilian brain, took over. When traumatic memories are triggered, survivors often resort to acting on instinct, which can be extremely helpful in life-threatening situations. Yet, these situations can also become harmful, especially when the survivor ends up shifting into different trauma reactions, which may present as seeking quick relief or any type of pseudo-safety, or engaging in some old, familiar, and unhealthy behaviors, which include suicidal ideations and self-harming behaviors. It is extremely difficult in those moments for the survivor to access the rational mind and think of the natural consequences while the traumatic brain is being triggered. Therefore, it invariably exposes survivors to further danger and further vulnerabilities. It may make sense then that survivors benefit greatly if unnecessary retraumatization can be avoided and prevented as much as possible. Retraumatization often leaves them at a complete loss and leads to serious negative consequences, because at the time survivors are being triggered, their present moment often collapses into their past.

As you can probably imagine, when complex trauma survivors begin their healing journey, they will have to deal with fragments of traumatic memories they have not been consciously aware of, meaning they will have to deal with repressed and dissociated aspects of their original trauma, which in many cases is very difficult. These memories were assigned emotional significance while under a great deal of stress and they are accompanied by the sensory components of the trauma. Therefore, when a trauma survivor gets in touch with these memories, they have to relive the event with all its important components, meaning they will be exposed to the pain that they originally escaped by using their defense mechanisms. Accepting traumatic memories and accepting all the different components of the self is a very frightening chapter, especially at the onset, because there is always that initial fear on the part of the survivor of wondering who they will become when all of the outer layers eventually get peeled off and they meet their authentic self.

What complex trauma survivors need more than anything is to be in a supportive environment where corrective experiences can take place, such as in a therapy session. Ideally, their families, friends, and support systems would use a trauma informed approach as well, because left to their own devices, unnecessary retraumatization only leads to more of the same, meaning more negativity and more emotional pain. Prolonged trauma has programmed survivors to use defense mechanisms that are not easily undone. They take a lot of strength, patience, and courage to eventually be adjusted and transformed. The more we can provide corrective experiences for complex trauma survivors the better we can facilitate the rewiring of their emotional brain, which is essential for their healing journey.

CHAPTER 9

TRAUMA AND DISSOCIATION

THE MAIN PSYCHOLOGICAL DEFENSES COMPLEX trauma survivors use in order to deal with their intense emotional, physical, and mental pain can be organized into two major classes of psychological defense mechanisms. One being different levels of cognitive distortions, and the other being different levels of dissociation. Cognitive distortions refer to a tendency of placing a self-enhancing spin on unfavorable events with the intent to lessen the impact of these experiences on the self and an attempt to cope with significant internal and external stress. They are a form of alteration and modification which are extremely common and include intellectualization, rationalization, repression, reaction formation, displacement, denial, and isolation. Extreme cognitive distortion can be found in psychotic states and can become more terrifying and frightening and promote more dysfunctional behavior in the individual, which is often expressed in the form of paranoid ideations and/or delusions (Bowins, 2004).

In this work, I will focus on the topic of dissociation as a major defense mechanism because I believe it is most prevalent in the narratives I share with the reader, which can be viewed as a form of a breakdown of psychological functioning and a modification of one's own self. It may be best explained as an internal move trying to divide the unbearable experiences into different, mostly unconscious parts of the body and mind so the core personality can survive the trauma and still be able to function on some level in everyday life. The fact that there is a high prevalence of various dissociative states, especially milder ones, in relatively healthy individuals, makes it plausible to assume that dissociation is in fact one of our major psychological defenses. With that defense mechanism in place, it explains that our life experiences become discontinuous, and as we look back at our life, we are often faced with the fact that our memory is full of black holes. This also explains why most complex trauma survivors are unable to give a complete narrative and have difficulty wrapping their head around their own narrative, because that process was so significantly disrupted (Bowins, 2004).

Dissociation is one of the defense mechanisms human beings apply when trying to protect themselves from any anxiety-provoking and/or threatening experience and is a crucial component in our everyday life when trying to maintain emotional homeostasis. Without these defense mechanisms our conscious mind would become too overwhelmed and too vulnerable to negatively charged emotions, which would render us incapacitated quickly. When severe emotions take over, such as fear, anxiety, and sadness, these psychological defense mechanisms serve us in our attempt to reduce the force or magnitude of the negative experience. Therefore, our main goal in such situations is to use dissociation to dampen the intensity, frequency, and duration of these negative emotions, so we may be able to maintain and or restore a healthy state of mind. Spontaneous dissociative experiences are found among all ages, socioeconomic levels, colors, and creeds. The ability to dissociate appears to be greater in our earlier life and lessens as we get older, and it appears that our ability to dissociate might be based more on endogenous factors, meaning it might be based on factors from within, rather than on psychosocial factors, meaning any situation in which both psychological and social factors are assumed to play a role (Lionetti, 2004).

Dissociation occurs on a continuum with normal dissociation, such as spontaneous dissociation, on one side of the spectrum and pathological dissociation, such as dissociative identity disorder, on the other side of the spectrum. Dissociation progressively intensifies anywhere from normal levels of dissociation (such as arriving at a destination and having no recall of part or all the journey, highway hypnosis, staring into space, missing part of a conversation, or becoming totally absorbed in a movie) all the way to pathological levels of dissociation (such as not remembering significant events like one's own wedding or the birth of one's own child, not remembering buying items in one's belongings, finding oneself dressed in clothes one does not remember buying or putting on, not recognizing oneself in the mirror, or meeting people who feel that they know us and call us by a different name). Again, in addition to having these experiences, it is very much a matter of intensity, frequency, and duration in which these dissociative experiences occur. Pathological dissociation means that these dissociative experiences become more frequent and more severe, and that they are more likely to interfere with an individual's level of functioning (Ross, 2013).

While those facts explain quite powerfully why we may react in irrational ways at the time, or why we may seem removed from reality, or why we may have difficulty staying present, these reactions and behaviors by themselves should not be used to label us as damaged goods and rule us as less credible in any sense of the word. Instead, it should give those around us a better understanding of the complexity of what we have survived, render them a bit more compassionate with us, and create a willingness in them to give us time to regroup—instead of putting more pressure on us or worse, dismissing us or discrediting us. De-escalation should be the key not only on the inside but also on the outside. It should make sense by now that our healing journey into the depth of our psyche does not just happen overnight, but instead often stretches out over years or even decades, because it involves so many complex layers of the self.

When we find ourselves emotionally overwhelmed, especially if the situation resembles any type of threat, our internal self-care system may step in and take matters in its own hand. Its goal is always to get our host or core personality away from the emotional pain and away from the imminent threat that we are facing at the time. When we move into fight, flight, or freeze mode, we are no longer capable of responding rationally or effectively, and our brain and body automatically reach for our defenses to cope with the significant stressor, which may resemble a repeat of the original trauma. If the attempt to withdraw fails, the internal self-care system may opt to take more serious steps, especially if we are unable to stop the threat. Again, it is important to remember, that our psychological defense system is expressed often unknowingly in each of us much like our immune system, which operates without our conscious awareness (Bowins, 2004).

While our coping mechanisms were vital for our survival, they are also extremely difficult to undo. They not only keep us protected from overwhelming emotional pain but create the basis of our understanding and inform us of the way we interpret life experiences. Stepping out of everyday life while another part of us takes over, even after we have escaped our trauma, comes at a high cost. Truth is, our coping mechanisms are often still at work long after we have escaped our psychological and physical torture or captivity. Until we learn that it is safe to stay present in the face of discomfort, learn to mange to no longer feel dead and numb inside, and begin to recognize that we may be somewhat equipped to live a full or peaceful life, we will resort to our old defense mechanisms, which have served us well, considering we are here to tell our story.

It takes time for our internal self-care system to trust that we will be capable of dealing with life in a much healthier fashion, that we will not end up in a repeat of the initial trauma, and that we can act like a team on the inside, which many of us have never experienced before. Our healing work consists of inviting our split-off parts, those detached fragments of our soul, to return and be reintegrated into the core personality, which is a very sacred and delicate process and takes time. Like rebuilding trust in our dealings with the outside world, we must also rebuild trust on the inside. Our internal self-care system must recognize we no longer need to go to these default settings, and we are indeed robust enough and experienced enough to respond to events and keep our thinking brain activated, which allows us to think things through, maintain perspective, and think of alternative solutions (Kalshed, 1996).

72

From a psychological perspective, our instinctive response to trauma is withdrawal, and when withdrawal on the outside is impossible, a part of our inside must be withdrawn, and our ego must split into fragments. Originally, the traumatic, overwhelming experiences had to be relegated to the body and banished to discrete psychic parts, between which amnestic barriers had to be erected, so the dissociated material was never returned to our consciousness. Trauma is basically a rupture of our life and our developmental transitions, which are not only incredibly important, but they make life worth living. Because we do not get to make these transitions, dissociation becomes the strategy, an archetypal defense used to create shelter for the soul. While these defenses allow for survival of affect, which simply cannot be processed with the normal resources available to a child, the psyche deploys these resources as a last resort, knowing they will block the ego's path to wholeness. Therefore, putting the fragmented pieces of our psyche back together is vital for survivors of complex trauma and is an essential part of our healing journey (Kalshed, 1996).

CHAPTER 10

TRAUMA AND ADDICTION

FOR SOME REASONS, DRUGS AND alcohol were never appealing to me as an option to cope with my pain for two reasons. First, I believe, because I witnessed and lived through all the ugly consequences of alcohol abuse by living with an alcoholic for all my years growing up. Second, I believe, because I was frequently drugged for the purpose of sexual abuse, and because coming off those drugs in combination with recovering from the injuries I sustained during the abuse was simply vile and not anything I was ever willing to repeat. To this day any altered mental status can easily trigger panic attacks for me. I was addicted to nicotine, though, and I clearly remember smoking my first cigarettes at age seven. I still remember feeling very confused and troubled, not knowing where to turn for help, and deciding to reach for cigarettes because they were so readily available in our household, until my habit was eventually discovered. This did not stop me from smoking, however, but it required me to find different means to purchase my own cigarettes, which then was not as difficult as it would be in this day and age. Considering that the secondhand smoke in our household never even left during my formative years and that it took me decades to finally overcome my addiction to nicotine, the fact my lungs still work properly is another blessing in my life for which I am extremely grateful.

I have been working with the topic of addiction as long as I have been working in the helping profession, because the majority of patients who present for therapy who are dealing with some type of trauma, also struggle with some type of addiction. Over the years, I saw so many people on the frontline in the Emergency Room, struggling with substance abuse issues, usually brought to the ER by law enforcement—sometimes even in handcuffs—because their addiction took hold of them. In the process of their intoxication they had become agitated or even acutely suicidal. Some had attempted to harm themselves. Others had threatened that they would harm themselves. Therefore, they were taken to the ER, because they were considered to be a danger to themselves. Others became extremely irritable and aggressive and were deemed dangerous to those around them, because they were unable to regulate their strong emotions and were about to cause harm. Some of them had assaulted others in the process, damaged property, or broken the law in some other way. Nevertheless, the first stop in all of these crisis situations was a visit to the ER to rule out any underlying medical conditions and allow for a safe detox and a safe sobering period.

Drugs and alcohol not only alter our mental status and momentarily help numb our pain, but they are also very disinhibiting. They can make us very irritable, aggressive, and in the long run make us more depressed, so any underlying passive suicidality or homicidality can become acute. I have been privileged to assess hundreds of patients dealing with substance abuse issues, and have met with people of all ages, cultures, socioeconomic status, gender, faith, and ethnicity, simply because addiction is not a respecter of any natural and or artificial boundaries, and neither are adverse childhood experiences. In general, these individuals are very reluctant to blame anybody or anything, because they realize they are old enough to take responsibility for their own behavior, which is, of course, an extremely important aspect in any type of recovery. As you can probably imagine, it takes some time interviewing an individual in crisis, especially if their mind has been altered, to get past the feelings of guilt, shame, and embarrassment for their often irrational behavior in connection with their substance abuse, to take an in-depth life events history. I have found that the trauma history itself is usually tucked far away, because the issues around the addictive behaviors have become pronounced and are causing interference and dysfunction in their everyday life. Often the individuals no longer make a conscious connection between the two.

Nevertheless, once sobered up, individuals who suffer from substance abuse are usually at a complete loss trying to understand why they cannot stop their addictive behaviors, even though they have made some serious attempts to stop their addiction. Their basic understanding is that the addictive behavior was genetically handed down to them, referring to the generation after generation in their family tree who struggled with the exact same issues. As they reflect deeper, they usually begin asking themselves how they have been able to change so many other negative aspects of their family history, but their substance abuse issue won't budge or go away. At those times, I would probe about their upbringing, which in most cases revealed their ACEs score—generally greater than four—and it became apparent that besides dealing with substance abuse, they were also dealing with long-term consequences of their original trauma. The combination of the two had made their lives even more complicated and complex.

I would share with them the research that was not only showing the connection between child maltreatment and substance abuse disorders, but also the fact that individuals who have been sexually, physically, and emotionally abused at an earlier age, experience more drug and alcohol abuse than individuals who have not. These adverse childhood experiences are likely correlated to their drug and alcohol dependency.

Furthermore, exposure to interpersonal violence, such as physical assaults or partner and family violence, at an early age have been associated with the highest risk for lifetime use of all drug types. It is estimated, in general, out of the approximately 26 million Americans who are addicted to some kind of substance, more than 60 percent report that they have experienced adverse childhoods, and that number is fairly stable, no matter what subgroup we focus on.

Current studies on addiction aim to understand how these scary, dangerous, and life-threatening childhood experiences in an individual's life affected their addiction development and susceptibility, and what variables might be responsible and may lead to a certain outcome. In this research, the focus is on the developing brain of a child and the fact that positive as well as negative encounters and conditions affect the small human brain and its ability to react and adjust to environmental stimuli, which is called brain plasticity. Again, these encounters can make or break, strengthen or weaken, and create or dispose of neural connections which are in charge of brain development. It is believed that childhood trauma and maltreatment are the cause of cognitive, social, and behavioral impairments, and that continuous pressure causes vulnerabilities which make the individual more likely to develop substance abuse disorders.

The opioid attachment-reward system, the dopamine-based incentive-motivation apparatus, and the self-regulating areas of the prefrontal cortex are all not functioning properly in addictive individuals. In addition, the stress-response mechanism has been deeply affected, because they are so exquisitely attuned to their environment. It makes sense then, that childhood maltreatment interferes with the ability to love, make connections, regulate pain as well as pleasure, manage incentives, and be able to be motivated. Looking at addiction from that angle, it certainly helps explain why individuals who are addicted to any substances are also struggling in so many other areas in their everyday life and why sobriety is so difficult to attain (Mate, 2012).

In one of the first studies conducted on addicted women and trauma, they found that addicted women have been sexually, physically, and emotionally abused by more perpetrators, more frequently, and for longer periods of time than their non-abused counterparts. They also found 74 percent reported sexual abuse, 52 percent reported physical abuse, and 72 percent reported emotional abuse, and the majority of addicted women have experienced sexual and/or physical abuse in their post-trauma life. In comparison, reports of incarcerated men show that about 50 percent of them experienced verbal abuse, 41 percent experienced physical abuse, 18 percent experienced sexual abuse, 18 percent experienced emotional neglect, and 12 percent experienced physical neglect. However, the long-term consequences of their childhood maltreatment generally

78

led to more violence in their teenage and early adulthood years, fueled by increased levels of aggression, self-destruction, and suicidal behaviors which were often exacerbated by the use of alcohol and drugs and were a precursor to their consequential incarceration (Ford, Barton, Newbury, Hughes, Bezeczky, Roderick, & Bellis, 2019).

So, in summary, it is important to understand that most addicts self-medicate to soothe their emotional pain, because their brain development was literally sabotaged by their traumatic experiences. The ongoing nature of the toxic stress levels and the serious disruption of their childhood development also lowered their stress threshold, meaning these individuals are triggered more easily and are more prone to experience anxiety and distress, which makes it more likely for them to reach for the substance.

These important facts should make it crystal clear that telling someone to stop their addictive behaviors and wanting them to just snap out of it is something that is simply physiologically and psychologically impossible. Furthermore, it should make it just as clear that focusing on the addiction alone is not enough, and that the original trauma and its long-term consequences need to be addressed simultaneously. It makes sense then, that lowered stress levels and ongoing positive experiences and lots of support, in conjunction with addiction- and trauma-focused treatment, are likely the most effective route to go.

While we are looking at the topic of trauma and addiction, I also want to look at sexual addictions, because that topic is even less understood in our society than the topic of substance abuse, especially in connection with trauma. I have worked with many, men in particular, who were sexually abused as children and/or adolescents, who ended up being addicted to pornography and masturbation. Even when the survivors of sexual abuse are in fulfilling and meaningful relationships, the sexual addiction does not necessarily go away. It so often causes a lot of pain and suffering for their partners as well as for themselves, because those addictive habits and behaviors are just as difficult to break as substance abuse, for example. It usually takes a lot of time, effort, and commitment, a good therapeutic relationship, as well as participating in support groups, and it can still average about four to five years of treatment for the individual to be able to establish sobriety, which can be very discouraging for the survivors and their partners alike.

I am speaking of the type of sexual addiction here that is caused by a traumatic childhood and by the fact that the individual was unable to form a secure attachment with his or her caregivers, which fits into the category of emotional neglect, and is experienced by the child as extremely traumatic. The disrupted attachment between the caregiver and the child in early childhood is usually not expressed or verbalized because of the inability of the individual to name or symbolize emotions and the inability to metabolize the event, which creates a deficit in the ability to modulate these emotions.

The child needs the co-regulation of emotions from the caregiver, especially when it comes to painful emotions. Addictive sexual behaviors can, in fact, be a dissociative defense mechanism used in an attempt to modulate traumatic memories triggered by stressful events. The process is not consciously understood by the individual, because the sexually addictive behavior is a mechanism that was designed to create a retreat from the traumatic emotions. Therefore, what we often find in individuals who are sexually addicted is an inability to recognize painful emotions and signals, their threshold for sensory stimuli has been altered, and their tolerance window for emotional stress has been narrowed, which often leads to severe levels of confusion, disorientation, and dissociation. Instead of judging these individuals, we need to help them gain clarity about their emotional experiences, and what it is that triggers them. Learning to think clearly and feel more clearly will eventually allow them to discover their own subjectivity, and the subjectivity in others, and it will help them, literally, to learn who they are, where they end, and where another person begins which is so essential for any of us (Craparo,2014).

CHAPTER 11

THE INTERNAL SELF-CARE SYSTEM

COMPLEX TRAUMA DURING CHILDHOOD, ESPECIALLY if it occurs as early as infancy, can be described as the total annihilation of the human personality and the destruction of the personal spirit. Because the trauma occurs before a coherent ego has been developed, and because coherent ego defenses have not yet been formed, psyche finds itself having to create another line of defenses, which is called the "second line of defenses," trying to prevent the unthinkable from being experienced on the conscious level, which would completely overwhelm the child. These defenses include splitting among multiple centers of identity, projective identification, depersonalization, and psychic numbing (Kalshed, 1996).

Again, while these defenses are life saving during the abuse, they often prove to be maladaptive later in life when the trauma is no longer occurring. Since not all created parts become benevolent in nature, but some of them become malevolent, they often create another abuse cycle on the inside and cause some self-destruction. Trauma research has also shown that some parts of the psyche regress to the infantile period and other parts of the ego progress, and they manage the adaptation to the outside world. By doing so, they become the "caretakers" of the regressed parts on the inside. Kalshed reminds us that the way the psyche uses fragmentation of consciousness, especially when trauma strikes early in a developing child, should not be taken for granted and instead, perhaps

81

we should acknowledge their sophistication and miraculous nature, which I very much appreciate. In fact, I have a deep gratitude for that second line of defense, because were it not for them, I believe most of us would not have been able to survive.

It is suggested by the Kleinian school of thought, that the extreme levels of frustration experienced by the child may lead to unbound rage, which if it does not find adequate expression toward the outside, might boomerang toward the ego itself, and eventually end up being expressed mercilessly on the inside, meaning the child might end up with an "internal agency of abuse." It explains to me clearly why we survivors often become our own worst enemy and why post-trauma life, paradoxically, can still be experienced as a living hell, because those benevolent and malevolent dynamics continue to stay in place until we get to a place in our healing journey where we have the opportunity as well as the appropriate resources to reintegrate those subconscious and unconscious parts of us.

Extreme traumatization leads to experiences in which the "skin-encapsulated ego" dissolves and survivors leave their bodies, and while they are in this type of a trans state, an observing ego becomes kind of a witness. This may be a key to understanding dissociation or other mechanisms that can result from traumatic experiences in which the individual eventually crosses boundaries between the material and physical world into this kind of no-man's-land or the immaterial world of consciousness. Wirtz calls this initiation into the unknown, in which one is robbed of the familiar structures, especially as a child, a state of disorientation and ambiguity where space and time no longer mean anything and where the child is full of agony, desperation, and confusion. The author calls this in between or liminal space the "Betwixt and Between," and I would like to call it the "Neither Here nor There" (Wirtz, 2014).

Having moved through these different realms for so long, wandering around in the twilight zone, feeling strangely familiar with the underworld, yet simultaneously still belonging to the reality of the upper world, some of us trauma survivors feel like wayfarers. When this bizarre journey becomes the place where we reside for a long period of time under such perilous conditions, it often feels that our soul has been murdered and has long left our physical body. In this state, we know intuitively that our soul cannot transition to the spirit world while our physical body is still alive, and it feels very much like our souls have become trapped in this sort of limbo. This may explain why we so often find ourselves in a constant state of falling apart and gathering back up the broken pieces in a constant battle between individuation and fragmentation, as a desperate attempt to regain some type of meaning for our life and somehow bring our soul back home. When the original trauma hits or when additional trauma is being experienced and our more primitive defenses fail, our secondary defenses or archetypal defenses will take over and try to go to any length to protect the self, even if that means that it would kill off the host personality and with that, the body in which the mind and spirit are housed (Kalshed, 1996).

Our secondary defenses, these archetypal defenses, are usually organized by a deeper center of the personality than the ego. To me, this often explains what may have gone on in the psyche of trauma survivors who have attempted or completed suicide, especially when loved ones ask what made the individual not remember their family member(s) and all the potentially good reasons they had to hold onto their post-trauma life. The best way I can verbalize the change that takes place on the inside in situations like that—like finding oneself in yet another horribly abusive situation without the slightest glimmer of hope for an escape—is that the inside simply decides to take over, desperately trying to protect the host or core personality from the overwhelming emotional pain. It is like being in a tunnel where we experience the past and present trauma combined, which prompts our system to go on autopilot, where the sole focus is on trying to overcome the enormous emotional pain, where our rational mind is no longer accessible or goes offline, and we have little or no control over what happens next on the inside.

Again, we have to remember that the internal self-care system is not only there to preserve and protect and act like a benevolent force, but it also gives rise to persecution and destruction, acting like a malevolent force, which becomes the internal antagonist

83

who is opposed to the enjoyment of life, happiness, and success, and instead aims for misery, unhappiness, and self-destruction. The overarching goal of the secondary or archetypal defenses then is to protect, preserve, and persecute in an attempt to keep "things on the inside" and out of reality.

CHAPTER 12

LEARNING FROM HUMAN EXPERIENCE

THE PHILOSOPHY I EMBRACE IN this work is based on the assumption that lived experience is an interpretive process that takes place in the individual's world. It can be beneficial for the researcher to reflect on the participant's experiences and simultaneously reflect on his or her own experience and by doing so, capture the nature and essence of the phenomenon in his or her written reflections, contributing to the ever evolving understanding of the essence of this particular phenomenon.

I feel that complex trauma and its long-term consequences are an appropriate topic for this type of inquiry, because it is all about a certain way of being in the world. Instead of bracketing myself off from the project, I am bringing my own personal experiences to the table while I am constantly exploring my own subjectivity and biases. Again, the way I designed this book, sharing my personal life experiences at the beginning, was to draw the reader into the important topic of unnecessary retraumatization, knowing these experiences are universal and experienced by countless others. I felt even more of an urgency to address the phenomenon at a time where we will see an unprecedented amount of post-traumatic reactions in our society due to the global pandemic we have all experienced with all its traumatic aspects, tremendous losses, and complicated layers of confusion and deception. While I am trying to show you the fullness and complexity of the topic, I am asking you for your attention, your open-mindedness, and your wonder to fully consider and receive the deep meaning of these shared experiences.

Phenomenological work is about bringing into nearness that which tends to be obscure and tends to evade the intelligibility of our natural attitude toward everyday life. The understanding of a phenomenon, such as lived experience, is not fulfilled with just knowing the facticity—meaning the circumstances of a particular experience—but it requires a thoughtful and reflective grasping of what it is that renders it significant. The goal of this inquiry is to bring to light the nature, significance, and essence of these experiences in a perhaps so far unseen way. It is a creative attempt to capture this way of life in an analytical and holistic, a unique and universal, and a powerful and sensitive way (Van Manan, 1990).

Because lived experience can neither be fully explained nor can it necessarily be categorized, I will provide you with interpretive descriptions of the varieties and possibilities, drawing from my own perspective and from the perspective of other survivors. My hope is that I can convey to the reader what it means to experience life from this post-traumatic angle and explain how difficult it is for some of us to shift structures of meaning and perception of our surroundings as quickly as our support systems would like us to, because these structures are so deeply embedded in our fabric of life. I wish to shed light onto the individual and the universal ways we as human beings tend to respond to the enormous pressures in our personal lives and how we develop coping mechanisms that allow us to somehow stay alive and help us manage to survive.

There are two main approaches to phenomenological inquiry, meaning the study of human experiences, one of them being transcendental or descriptive phenomenology, and the other being hermeneutic or interpretive phenomenology. Transcendental phenomenology asks the researcher to stand back and to keep his or her bias and preconceived notions in check and out of the research itself. The hermeneutic approach assumes that a human researcher cannot experience a phenomenon without referring back to his or her own personal experience. Furthermore, in hermeneutic phenomenology the researcher's past experiences and the researcher's knowledge are valuable guides to the phenomenological inquiry. Here it is the researcher's education that leads him or her to the phenomenon. This phenomenological approach requires the researcher to read deeply into the inquiry and to try to grasp the wholeness project via thinking and writing (Neubauer, Witkop, and Varpio, 2019).

Since experiences of the numinous, which is in general defined as an experience that makes you fearful as well as fascinated, awed yet attracted, and overwhelmed but also inspired, seems to only be satisfactorily described in the form of a narrative, I have chosen to share the following narratives. It is my intention to remain open to the human experiences as they present themselves and to look for the essence of the experiences without imposing my own opinion onto them, because I believe they carry the seed of transformation within them. The topic by itself is involved and draws on our spiritual energy and personal courage for everybody involved. And I hope and pray that it will not only increase our understanding and compassion, but that it will also have the power to heal hearts of survivors and non-survivors alike (Van Manan, 1990).

As far as my own spiritual journey is concerned, I dove headfirst into a church just prior to the time I was finally able to begin my healing journey, hoping to find some normalcy and comfort in a religious organization. I was hoping to offer something to my children that had not been given to me when I grew up that would allow them to develop some faith in God and to have a foundation on which to build our little family. It actually worked for some time, until I found out for myself that my new church family had many flaws and there was a lot of hypocrisy and darkness. But when I unfortunately witnessed some people around me who were getting hurt under the umbrella of Christianity, again by deep and dark family dynamics that were neither stopped nor allowed to be discussed, I could no longer be part of that family system, either. At first that was rather devastating for me, but as time went on, I found my own path of spirituality and developed a personal relationship with God. My studies in Depth Psychology were a life saver because I was able to expand my spirituality, and I was also able to make some sense of what happened. I am grateful that I could overcome the loss of my second family, though it did set me back significantly and created some psychological turmoil. I thankfully had enough tools to avoid being totally thrown off my path, and instead I was able to learn from those difficult experiences and continue with my trauma recovery.

My personal experience is again not as unique as you might think, because many complex trauma survivors have unfortunately experienced similar dynamics in their search for spirituality. Carl G. Jung actually states in his work that almost all the patients he worked with eventually ended up looking at their purpose of life in the latter part of their therapy, and it shifted the focus of the treatment to an in-depth look at the topic of spirituality. It gave me comfort and inspired me to continue with my spiritual journey, despite the fact that I had landed once again in an abusive family, and it was not necessary to assign fault to me. (C. G. Jung, 1963).

What I came upon in my studies was the fact that we human beings have the unique ability to learn from other people's mistakes, and at the same time we are also very unique in being resistant to do so. It is interesting to me that when we humans come across a narrative that we cannot relate to, we might think that life would not place us into a similar situation, which can easily make us judgmental. Perhaps we assume that we surely would have responded differently and would have made wiser decisions, which is so easy to do if we are not in that particular situation, or we might believe that the subjective experience of another person is not very reliable data and may disregard the narrative all together. Regardless what our reasons may be, I believe it is essential for all of us to postpone that type of judgment, because it serves us to learn from the experience of others so that we can all achieve new understanding and glean new insights into lived experiences simply for the betterment of humanity (Neubauer, Witkop, and Varpio, 1963).

The fact that knowledge does not end with connectedness and understanding, but in general, it opens up additional insight into more meaning, truth, and essence along the way, and it opens up other journeys within journeys within journeys. The beauty of knowledge and discovery, therefore, is that it keeps us very much alive, awake, and connected, which I believe we need more and more of as a society in this rather challenging season. With that being said, I feel ready to share the narratives of those survivors who graciously gave me permission to share their life experiences, solely in hopes that it will serve a greater purpose—that we might beat the odds and in fact learn from each other's experiences, especially for the purpose of future generations (Moustakas, 1994).

As per Brenee Brown, in *The Atlas of the Heart*, If we want to find the way back to ourselves and one another, we need language and the grounded confidence to both tell our stories and be (good) stewards of the stories that we hear. Furthermore, the author adds that she feels that that is the framework for meaningful connection (Brown, 2021).

PART 3

CHAPTER 13

NARRATIVE # 1

THIS YOUNG WOMAN HAD BEEN through a season in her life, post her adverse childhood, where she had raised children and been rather content. From what I gathered, she enjoyed motherhood, and her children developed and became great individuals in their young adult life.

When her children left the home, she was back on her own, and she was completely caught off guard when someone close to her family romantically maneuvered himself into her life. For a moment it felt good to have someone admire her, but that honeymoon phase quickly wore off, and she began realizing she was stuck in an abusive relationship. It did not look like there was an easy way out. As the abuse became increasingly more violent, she realized it was triggering her complex-trauma issues related to the abuse from her past, which she thought she had long put behind herself. She struggled to come up with a solid plan to safely get out of the situation. But by now she had learned she was dealing with a felon who was capable of extremely violent acts and had very little regard for others, including herself. He had been in and out of jail or prison for most of his adult life, had extreme anger issues, and had become more and more agitated and more unstable as time went on. One day some detectives showed up at their home and he was arrested on some prior charges. The woman thought it may provide the perfect opportunity to develop a plan to escape, unfortunately, he was released within days after his arrest, and he was right back where he had left off. A few months later he was booked into jail on yet another charge, but he called just a day later because he was being released, and he demanded a ride home. By then she had gained more clarity about the seriousness of her situation, and she had grown tired of constantly being abused.

On their way home, they got into an altercation, fueled by the fact that the man was feeling sorry for himself and was completely unwilling to take any type of responsibility for his actions. As things escalated, her passenger suddenly reached over, trying to yank on the steering wheel. She decided to slam her arm down as hard as she could, attempting to loosen his grip. Because that maneuver was unsuccessful, she decided to use her drag-racing skills to her advantage, in hopes to expel the immediate threat from the car. Unfortunately, the car she was driving responded very differently from what she had hoped, and the car ended up hitting the middle divider head on at a high speed. What happened next is a bit of a blur for her, but she recalls that the car went straight up into the air, and then ended up bouncing along the freeway until it finally came to a stop. At that point, the car was lying on its roof, with her hanging upside down in her seat belt. As she was trying to orient herself, she happened to see her abuser walking up and down the shoulder, speaking on his cell phone—unscathed—while it was very clear to her that she was seriously injured. She later learned she had shattered her wrist trying to fend off her passenger's attempt to take over the steering wheel, which caused her to lose control over the vehicle. And she learned that she had broken her neck in the accident, and her plan to get rid of the man next to her had not only failed, but she had almost been killed in this tragic accident.

The rescue workers told her that it was a miracle she was still alive, and they quickly transported her to the nearest trauma center. She underwent multiple surgeries, and when she came to and opened her eyes, who else but her abuser was sitting at her bedside. At this point she was wearing a post-surgery halo, and she was completely defenseless, meaning she was dependent on assistance 24/7. She tried to assert herself as soon as she could and alert the staff at the hospital to the fact that she was in an abusive relationship, and that the man sitting at her bedside was the very reason why she had almost died in the car accident. Some of them listened and even tried to create a safer environment for her by asking him to leave the room. When her treatment in the hospital came to an end, she was released back home into the 24/7 care of her abuser, since our medical system is not exactly prepared to deal with such precarious situations, and there really are no good alternatives.

Within months there was another altercation that ended up with her in the Emergency Room, at which point she finally decided to seek a temporary restraining order. But now she had to deal with the backlash of reporting the domestic violence to the authorities, because the man was not only trying to ignore her claims, but he was also assuming that he was above the law. Therefore, he was unwilling to leave the home. In one of his fits of rage, he happened to assault another person in public, causing such physical damage that the person filed charges against him, which put him finally back into jail. It was a strange blessing in disguise, because this incident finally enabled her to execute her getaway, and she was able to escape the relationship for good.

REFLECTIONS

At this point you may ask yourself, how come the person made it out of the original abuse, raised great children as a single mom, made a life for herself professionally, and then found herself in an abusive relationship later in life? Again, simply because the original abuse has subsided does not mean the complex dynamics of that trauma have all been undone. Having children changes our focus dramatically, because it keeps us busy trying to do the best we can to create a healthy environment and make sure that our children get to grow up and have a better life than we had. But that does not mean we have been able to heal from all our wounds.

Let's go back and visit her original trauma for a moment, which took place during her childhood and teenage years, where her mom initially took the brunt of the abuse. She and her siblings frequently witnessed their father, in his drunken stupors, beat Mom so badly that she and her siblings never knew if mom would be alive the following day. Slowly but surely, as she and her siblings grew older, her father's physical and emotional abuse was no longer solely focused on mom, but they all became targets for his rage. She feels that she must have reminded him of her mom, because looking back it seemed that she received substantially more abuse than her fair share. Keep in mind, her mother was being abused by the person who was supposed to love and care for her, and she was never able to get herself out of the abuse nor was she able to protect her own offspring from it. As her same-sex child grew up with the same type of abuse, she feels that, inadvertently, she became like her mom. She had an unhealthy role model of what healthy relationships looked like, so she never learned to set and maintain healthy boundaries, and she neither felt deserving nor did she ever learn how to say NO to abuse.

Again, as complex trauma survivors we usually have difficulties choosing partners that are good for us or knowing who to trust and how to look out for ourselves. We don't know who we really are at the core, what we are deserving of, or how to develop and/or maintain any type of healthy boundaries. All we really learned as we were growing up was how to survive abuse. We learned how to try to make it in the world, and generally, we do not ask for much. Many of us, at one point or another, have taken in friends or family members because they were in dire straits, including some of our non-protective parents and even our abusive parents. I believe we may feel obligated to do so, because we were able to escape the abuse and we were able to make some kind of a life for ourselves, despite what we had to endure. Therefore, some of us might feel obligated, and considering that we already took care of our parents emotionally while we were growing up, we are accustomed to being in that caretaker role.

I am sure you can imagine that does not always work out for the better of anyone involved. Though we may still be filled with resentment and experience many conflicting emotions—since most of us are caring people and do not want to perpetuate the cruelties that were done to us—instead of being able to say NO to such a request, we end up saying YES, even if it does not serve us well. In her case, the troubled person came to her because he had ended up incarcerated over and over again, as a consequence of his horrible childhood, and he begged and pleaded with her to give him a chance and help him get his life in order.

So, the two ended up in a relationship—basically by default—because both of them struggled with similar issues from their original trauma, but things began to take a turn for the worse. As both of them struggled with poor sense of self and difficulties modulating their emotions, one retreated inside and shut down, while the other one became more and more aggressive and eventually violent. This led to her being kept hostage in her home or in her car and pulled into more and more drama and chaos. She realized that not only was her sanity at risk, but as the violence continued to escalate, her own life was threatened.

The utter helplessness and the serious danger inherent in that situation, including her serious injuries, triggered all her original trauma. Though she eventually escaped her abuser, and though she survived her near-fatal car accident, she still needed to leave the area to be safe. With that she could no longer hold up her job and provide for herself the way she used to, and because her mental health deteriorated significantly, she needed to make time to solely focus on her complex-trauma recovery.

NARRATIVE # 2

ERE IS A DIFFERENT SCENARIO that still holds some similarities. Imagine yourself growing up in a minority family that is holding on to some rigid traditional, cultural, and religious values. At a rather early age, one of your parents decides to leave the religious traditions and instead dives into radical evangelism, and of course expects you to make the religious change with them. You are old enough to know that you are uncomfortable in the new church, which is an even stricter setting than the first church you attended. You take a stance, at nine years old, that you do not feel comfortable in the new setting, and you tell your parents that you choose not to go there anymore. Not only do you fall out of grace, but as the years go on you become this abhorrent and disgraced child in the overly religious parents' eyes. You are reminded repeatedly that God could not possibly love you and accept you because of your horrid personality and who you are at your core. So much for your innocence as a child and so much for your important development as a pre-teen and teen, as far as developing interests, developing views on life, choosing friends and a peer group, and especially developing your sexuality.

In this narrative, the young woman eventually stepped out and created a double life in her early teens because the oppression in her home became too much for her to deal with. While she maintained her daily life as far as attending her school and completing her chores, she began to sneak out of the house to meet up with her friends, who struggled with similar family dynamics and needed to break out because home was too toxic for them. These wounded and like-minded peers—who were either gay, lesbian, queer, or asexual and whose experience meant they clearly felt they did not belong with their biological families—understood each other and created strong bonds with one another. They accepted each other for who they were, they looked out for each other, and consequently these friends became her new family. Since this kind of night life for troubled teenagers, in general, is an attempt to cope, it naturally included drugs and alcohol—a lot of it—and of course early sexual experiences. This young woman recalls many close encounters where things could have gone very, very wrong.

Unfortunately, this young woman experienced a significant loss during those few years, which she could not possibly process or deal with in any healthy way because of her ongoing abuse at home and because she had to keep her dual life hidden. Her trauma, unfortunately, includes the death of a very close friend who had injected himself with enough heroin to make sure that his overdose would be fatal. The reason for his suicide, as he explained in his note, was the fact that he could no longer deal with the pain at home, which included ongoing severe mental, emotional, and physical abuse simply because he was so different and his parents were unwilling to accept him for who he was and because of his asexuality, his ongoing addiction, and his failed rehab attempts. Additionally, he felt that he had become too much of a burden to his friends, who he had trusted with the extent of his incredible internal pain. His tragic death spiraled his close friends into even deeper levels of depression and anxiety, and at first, they tried to cope with the overwhelming pain by drinking and using drugs even more heavily. Finally, a few of them sat down and re-evaluated their lives, and they decided to stop their self-destruction, so that they could honor their late friend's legacy, so that his life had not been taken in vain.

When this young woman pulled herself out of her double life, she had to face her everyday struggles in her abusive home life without her peer support group and her familiar ways of coping. On top of it, she was left with huge amounts of guilt and pain— pain surrounding the loss of her one friend who she felt completely understood by and who had been kind, gentle, and nurturing to her. This was on top of the layers of guilt and shame she was already suffering because of her mother's condemnation regarding her being sexually active and having relationships with other females. At that time, she had learned that any efforts on her part toward goodness were never good enough, because they did not align with godliness, since she did not have the same beliefs as her mother.

She did her best not to let on how much she was suffering at the time, but her eccentric evangelical parent noticed a significant shift in her behavior and decided to zero in on her suspicion that her offspring clearly must be living a sinful life because she was so visibly unhappy. She proceeded to bombard her with questions and accusations, and eventually forced her out of the closet as a lesbian. Little did anybody know what she was really struggling with. Though it was painful to be outed to her whole family and friends so prematurely and to be told daily that she was surely going to hell, it was a lot easier to deal with that than to deal with what was really burdening her. There was never any room to process the real trauma and the real pain, the loss of her dear friend, her own suicidality, and the fact that she had lived a double life ... until many years later.

She managed to graduate from high school on time with excellent grades, because school was what kept her going. She went to a junior college where she got several associate degrees before she transferred to a four-year university. And while she was focusing on her academics, she built another career, which supported her while continuing her education, all while her verbal and emotional abuse was at an all-time high. She realized that she needed to gain greater independence, though she had postponed getting her driver's license for as long as she could, because she was not very fond of driving in the first place. Just weeks after she passed her test in preparation for driving to and from the university she was transferring to, she was in a serious car accident because another driver rear-ended her, causing serious damage to the car, as well as to her. She sustained injuries that required her to take heavy-duty painkillers and undergo intensive physical therapy for more than a year. Eventually she decided to stop taking painkillers because she experienced serious adverse side effects and feared becoming addicted to heavy opioids.

The driver who caused the accident was not only unapologetic and aggressive at the accident scene, but he and his legal counsel accused her of faking her injuries, even in court, where she was called a liar, an opportunist, and many other choice words. Truth is that her chronic pain to this day keeps her from being able to sit or stand for extended periods, which makes academic studies and trying to make a living in the fitness profession rather difficult. Her chronic pain shows up unpredictably and relentlessly, even in her sleep, and not only interrupts her sleep pattern but also the quality of her everyday life. To this day, driving is still a source of great stress and anxiety, especially when she encounters a driver who seems to have very little regard for others, at which point she still has a fight-or-flight response, which makes her feel like wanting to jump out of her own skin.

REFLECTIONS

It does not always have to be what happened to us that becomes most traumatizing, but it can be what did *not* happen to us, which becomes most unbearable and most traumatizing. Secure attachments are a fundamental need and are necessary for our sense of safety and survival during our developmental years. Praise and encouragement are the fuel that allows us to test, experiment with, and explore the outside world. They allow us to learn and grow through new-world experiences, and they enable us to develop levels of confidence and independence. Without those secure attachments we are not only left to our own devices, but we are also left with a serious level of confusion and other complex issues. The reason why we cannot resolve any of them is because we simply do not have the physical, mental, and emotional capacity yet at such an early age.

It is a difficult and precarious situation to be confronted with knowing we need our caregiver for survival and, on the other hand, having to defend ourselves against the abuse by that very same caregiver. To negotiate this horrific conflict, we learn to dissociate the unacceptable feelings that rise on the inside, such as feelings of betrayal, terror, helplessness, loss, grief, and rage. Instead of being able to resolve them, we learn to deny them and detach from them, so that we can maintain some type of attachment to the caregiver, because without them our survival is seriously threatened. As you can imagine, it is not unusual to end up with idealized love for the caregiver on one hand, and with vengeful hatred for the same caregiver on the other hand, or any other combination in between (Ross and Halpern, 2009).

The adversity a child faces, does not have to be severe abuse to create deep, bio-physical changes. The ten different types of adversity examined in the ACEs study were almost considered equal, as far as the damage they can cause. Recurrent humiliation and ongoing put downs by a parent can have a slightly more detrimental impact and are marginally correlated with a greater likelihood of long-term consequences, meaning poorer outcomes of adult medical and mental health, than let's say physical health of a child. Dr. Nakazawa states that even chronic parental discord, the quiet divorce between two seething parents, and the early exit of a parent from a child's life, which happens in too many families, are all precursors to the same biochemical changes deep in the child's brain (Nakazawa, 2021).

NARRATIVE # 3

WHEN I MET THIS YOUNG woman for the very first time, I remember listening to her narrative and being appalled when she reported that her parents split up and both had moved out by the time she was eleven years old. Unfortunately, she had grown up in a drastically dysfunctional family. Her father had moved out first after a huge drama where her mom confronted her father's mistress, and she remembers the two women ending up in a physical fight. The father separated the two, but he ended up choosing the other woman over his family, and he moved out when she was ten years old. For the next year, her father harassed her mother endlessly, and finally one day he came over to the house and beat her mother. All the siblings went for cover, and when the fight was over and they felt safe to come out into the main part of the house, they realized that both their father and their mother were no longer in the house.

Since the mother did not return for the next four months, the young woman was afraid that her father had killed her—because she knew that her father was very capable of such a violent act—or that her mother may have committed suicide. As the oldest female child, she automatically ended up in charge of looking after the house, preparing meals, doing the laundry, and getting her younger siblings off to school in the morning and ready for bed at night. All her father was paying for was the mortgage and the utilities, and he dropped off weekly groceries which were never enough to feed everybody in the house, so, she decided to get her first job as a babysitter, to add to the household income and provide adequate food and clothing, and she has been working ever since.

Unfortunately, even before the parents left, there had been sexual abuse in the home, and consequently after they had left, she was sexually assaulted by her older sibling, but now even more frequently. A teacher noticed a change in her behavior and her alarming weight loss in a short period, and she spoke to the young woman. The teacher reported to child protective services as well as law enforcement, who got involved immediately. Unfortunately, though, the whole family was put in one room for questioning and follow-up, which made it impossible for the truth to come out. The young woman was threatened by her father before the family meeting and she was forced to lie, so when it came to the sexual-abuse allegations, she told the social workers that she had lied, and consequently all charges were dropped. After the official investigation, she received a severe beating from her father and he reiterated to her to never ever make a report no matter what was happening to her, which unfortunately stuck with her for a very long time, setting her up for more and more abuse. After the meeting, both parents went on their way, and she was back in charge of the household, and as provider for everybody who was left of the family unit. Her older sibling continued with the sexual abuse and her younger siblings were acting out and making her life extremely difficult for her.

Not having any guidance and still being naïve and vulnerable as a pre-teen and teen, led to many situations in which she was taken advantage of. She recalls witnessing a graphic sexual assault when she and her friend went to a party at someone's house. At one point she realized she had not seen her friend for a while, so she began searching for her. She ended up on the second floor, where she found her friend lying on a bed, completely unconscious, and she saw a bunch of teenage boys taking turns raping her friend's limp body. When she decided to sexually engage with boys herself, she summarizes that she had many horrific experiences, and just ended up "meeting more and more pigs."

REFLECTIONS

After raising her own family, and after deciding a few years back to do some honest healing work, she was very fortunate to find an amazing trauma therapist. To this day she feels that "you are just never safe, not even in close relationships." She feels that she will forever have her guard up, and that she will never get rid of her need for self-protection, which she feels has been her strength and her superpower. She describes herself as a "woman of steel," referring to the new strength which she feels she acquired on her journey, going literally through hell and back.

When she finally was brave enough to confront her dad way into her adult life and share with him that she had been sexually violated in her youth on many occasions, he responded by saying that everybody gets sexually violated, and he had been violated by his priest. She was trying to make him understand that what she was sharing with him was not about him, but that this was about her. She wanted to ask him where he was when she needed his protection. Unfortunately though, all she got from him was denial, minimization, and defensiveness. It only added to what she had already gathered throughout her post-trauma years, namely that people do not want to hear what she has to say. She states that she is tired of not being believed, being minimized, having people wanting to compete with her by stating that they had it much worse than her, or having to deal with people being disgusted and put off when they hear only part of her story, and especially people wanting to argue with her about her own narrative.

This young woman endured a very tough journey to get to the place where she is today, and she counts her blessings that her intrusive thoughts and memories are no longer all-encompassing, and no longer get the best of her. She is grateful that now she can choose what she wants to disclose, and who she is disclosing these things to. What she desires from those around her is that they show her they are trustworthy, and they are willing to give her the benefit of the doubt.

The natural consequences of such trauma include feeling profoundly damaged and alone, developing a deep sense of helplessness, and developing a core belief that nothing will ever work out all right. Such traumatic circumstances are simply not within the realm of normal human experiences, and the recovery from such complex trauma is not only very difficult but also very different from the experience of those around us, which singles us out even more.

NARRATIVE # 4

ET ME WALK YOU THROUGH another scenario of a young man who grew up in a very religious household. He remembers his years in elementary and middle school being completely overshadowed by sexual abuse from older boys. His earliest memory dates to when he was between four and five years old and was sexually molested by an older boy at a neighbor's house, which took him decades to uncover that specific memory entirely. When he recently spoke to his sisters about his sexual abuse history, and when he mentioned the location where the abuse took place, not only did they confirm the particular surroundings he remembers, but they also confirmed the oldest boy of that family being very troubled. The boy's sibling, all girls, who his older sisters had babysat, had all shown bizarre behavior in line with symptoms of early sexual abuse. Another memory, that is not as clear but seems to be just as troublesome, is about his baptism at the age of eight, which is coupled with another inappropriate incident in the locker room involving an older male that left him equally horrified and full of shame.

He recalls that he had gotten into a lot of trouble as early as kindergarten for either masturbating or trying to get under girls' skirts, and that he was suspended many times in elementary school, because he was just not able to stop his behavior. It was a huge relief for him to learn during his treatment that he was acting out because he had been sexualized so prematurely, and that it is not unusual for a child to display these behaviors. As a pre-teen he was exposed to pornography by his peers, which he feels made things only worse for him, and later he was seduced by an older boy whenever their families got together, and all the kids would have a sleepover. He felt horrible about himself, and between the bullying, the forbidden sexual activities, and confusion, he simply shut down. Over time, he became convinced that he was just a horrible, overly sexual person.

Consequently, he stayed away from girls throughout his teenage years, because he felt that girls would clearly not be interested in somebody as "disgusting" as him.

Because his family was so active in the church they belonged to, he not only had to attend the services during all those years, but he was also given responsibilities depending on his age. He states that those times were some of the worst in his life, trying to serve God while carrying around his big secret he felt he could not ever reveal. While he tried to spare his family from any consequences of his sinful behavior, he felt like he was going to melt away on the inside at any given moment. He felt like he was only a shell walking around, and he was so surprised to find that, after working through all the trauma, there was a real person underneath it all. He really has no conscious recall as far as when the abuse stopped, and he could no longer tell when he was abused and at what time he became a "willing participant or whatever he was." It should not come as a surprise that he often, to this day, completely shuts down and dissociates.

He felt so guilty and was dealing with so much shame on the inside that he had a hard time functioning at all during those years. His peers picked up on him being withdrawn and acting different-ly, and they mercilessly bullied him. He remembers coming home from school one day when he was about six or seven years old, and he panicked so badly when he realized that his parents were not home that he ended up calling 911. This was during a time where he was being molested by another neighbor, and he has no recollec-tion of what might have happened leading up to his panicked reac-tion that day. He remembers being completely terrified at finding himself home alone, and he could not think of anything else but to call the sheriff's department.

REFLECTIONS

The gentleman was sexually abused as early as four or five years old, by some children in his neighborhood, and he knew that he could not turn to his parents, because he did not have a secure attachment and because his caregivers were not attuned to his needs. The few times he tried to open up, he learned quickly that there was no compassion, understanding, or tolerance for any behavior outside the box. He recalls being scolded and told that he better snap out of his behavior because it was completely unacceptable in his hyper-religious household. Nevertheless, trying to deal with the ongoing abuse, he developed his addictive behaviors early on, and it apparently did not occur to his caretakers that he was dealing with traumatic experiences and clearly needed help. He was left to his own devices, and he states that he became that awkward kid that ended up being bullied for most of his middle-school years, on top of suffering sexual abuse in the neighborhood, which continued for a long time.

His post-trauma life has been difficult. Not only did he experience a complete mental break in his early twenties, but he also had a serious suicide attempt, which landed him in a mental-health unit about a decade later. While hospitalized, he was able to tell his story for the first time and process some of it, but it left him with intense feelings of guilt and shame, and his loved ones in even greater despair. When he entered therapy with a trauma therapist years later, he slowly came to understand the dynamics of his complex trauma and its long-term consequences. He was able to begin processing his pain, anguish, and his ongoing passive suicidality, and learn how to work with it more effectively. Here he was a grown man, who essentially did not know who he was and how to deal with life, other than to go through the motions. He was convinced, after all these years, that he had to just accept the fact that he had to live a painful and chaotic life.

Eventually, he realized that when difficulties arose, he would automatically leave his body and mind, by dissociating, and that was the time when his sexually addictive behaviors would rear their heads, which he had no control over, but left him feeling even worse about himself. In general, little is known about sexually addictive behaviors as a dissociative mechanism designed to help with managing traumatic memories triggered by stressful events. His comment that "he is not sure when his sexual abuse actually stopped and when he became a willing participant, or whatever it was that he became" was simply heartbreaking for me to hear. He eventually began realizing his difficulty with affect regulation, and that he had a hard time discerning what other people's intentions were, as well as being able to identify what his own intentions were. His sexual abuse started at a time in his young life when he should have been learning how to mentalize negative and painful emotions, meaning that he should have learned to symbolize and verbalize his traumatic experience with help of his caretakers.

It was a huge undertaking for him to decide to go into therapy, which was rather terrifying for him, and he had understandably put it off for as long as he possibly could. It reminded me of how hesitant and terrified I was to enter therapy, and I know that so many complex trauma survivors have felt or are still feeling very much the same. Many of us have been told for a lifetime that we are crazy by our abusers and have internalized that belief over time. So, entering therapy is pretty much about getting confirmation that something is wrong with us, and what we have been told for half of our lives and what we eventually told ourselves for the other half of our lives is simply true. It is scary to share our narrative, with a complete stranger, and it is even more terrifying to dive into the unknown and to look at all the aspects we do not want to look at within ourselves, meaning our shadow aspects. Because, what if therapy actually confirms that we are a misfit or a mistake, and what if that would wipe out that ever so slight glimmer of hope, that we are still holding onto somewhere, for our future. Then what?

NARRATIVE # 5

THIS SCENARIO TAKES PLACE IN a home where the parents were fighting constantly, and the young woman stated that her foundation for her upbringing was established while she was surrounded by ongoing domestic violence in the home. Her earliest memories include her hiding deep in the corner of her closet, and she remembers thinking early on that she was simply a mistake and that everything was basically her fault. She describes the atmosphere as terrifying and extremely toxic, and she remembers that in later years she would take her younger siblings into the closet with her. She stated that the issues were never resolved, and she and her siblings spent their whole childhood in this toxic environment. At about age eight, she recalls that she and her mother were visiting with a school psychologist. She remembers her mother being told that it was better for her child to be removed from public school because she was somewhat delayed and would not be able to perform at the level of her peers.

Consequently, the young girl was taken out of public school and home schooled by her mom, which not only took her away from all her peers, but she also no longer had any relief from the toxicity in her home. She feels that she grew up under a glass dome, where she was not only sheltered but also isolated from the outside world, deemed inadequate and programmed not to have any expectations whatsoever for any kind of future for herself. Apparently, the family funds were somewhat mismanaged, and the family lost their home and had to move to a scary neighborhood. The new house was rodent infested, soiled, and basically destroyed. At this time, the young woman was a pre-teen and she felt not only hopeless and helpless, but she also succumbed to the fact that there was nothing she could do, and there was no way for her to ever feel normal. From then on, she reports having a fear of losing everything. She no longer trusted people, and she did not have a good sense of humanity and she describes herself as a deer in headlights, perhaps the same way she felt at age eight when she received such a poor outlook and prognosis.

She states that there were so many occasions when she decided in her head that she wanted to end it all, because she felt super stressed all the time, and she became very depressed, but she did not follow through with any of her plans because she did not want to hurt another person. She managed to leave her home in her early adulthood. What she regrets the most is that she did not have a chance to be surrounded by her peers and she was never able to develop any social skills because of that. She ended up moving from place to place and had to learn to be by herself. Eventually she became extremely overwhelmed and depressed. She ended up in an inpatient mental-health facility, voluntarily, because she felt suicidal. She was eventually diagnosed with major depression and anxiety. She is most grateful for the program because it was there the seed was planted that what she had experienced throughout her childhood was simply not her fault, and for the first time in her life she started to embrace that idea.

REFLECTIONS

Much later, when she happened to work with a trauma therapist, she learned that what she was dealing with was in fact complex trauma, and her levels of depression and anxiety were natural consequences of her human experience. Today, she looks back on her life and at the price she had to pay for her original trauma, and she wishes she could have developed some tools while she was growing up that would have enabled her to deal with the micro dramas—trivial things in life—rather than still having them trigger major reactions and create major events for her, even as an adult. Because she had been living for so long in self-isolation and withdrawal, and because she grew up in such a toxic environment, it made it hard for her to manage a life without her old, imposed restrictions which had kept her back for such a long time. And though she has made tremendous progress in her recovery, on some level she is still dealing with that to this day.

After she had been treated for severe depression, it became clear to her that there was something else going on. It took a number of years until she ended up with a trauma therapist, who helped her understand that besides dealing with depression and anxiety, she was dealing with the long-term consequences of her complex trauma. It helped her understand what she had been wrestling with every day of her life, even after she escaped the original trauma. What stuck with her the most for so many years was that she had been treated as frail and in need of extra protection from the outside world, so she felt that she should never set any expectations to accomplish anything in life.

One day she decided to sign up for some college classes, and she was extremely surprised when she earned A's for her work, even though these were academically challenging classes. But because of her old mental tape, she was simply too afraid to pursue an academic career, and she quickly went back to what was familiar—back into her isolation and withdrawal. It took her a long time to accept that she might, in fact, be as intelligent as her therapists insisted, and that she could accomplish things she always thought of as out of her reach. At this point in her life, she states that she honestly believes the sky's the limit, which is heartwarming to hear.

NARRATIVE # 6

THIS NARRATIVE IS, UNFORTUNATELY, NOT as unusual as we would like to think. Anybody who knew this Brady Bunch family felt it was completely safe to send their own kids over for play time. Little did people know that there was a pedophile living in the home who sexually abused his little daughter for many years. Her first concrete memory dates back to about four years old, and yet she has suspicions that things may have started a lot sooner. While she feels she has implicit memory, she does not have declarative memory from anything prior to being about four. She recalls her father asking her to come into his bedroom while she was very young and stay with him while he was watching porn. She remembers not really understanding what she was watching. She felt very uncomfortable and wanted to go back to her room and play with her toys, but her father demanded that she stay.

Bad things only happened if her mom was working at her job and her older siblings were in school; therefore, nobody else in her family had a clue. The sexual inappropriateness took another turn when her father began coming into her room at night, frequently, to molest her until she was in her teenage years. Asked what she would do when these things happened, she stated that she would pretend to be asleep and that she would basically check out, meaning she would leave the scenario, internally, and to this day she uses a lot of dissociative defense mechanisms, even though she is in a healthy relationship in which she feels safe.

When she was sixteen and she had a steady boyfriend, everything took quite a turn, because once she told her boyfriend about what had happened throughout her whole upbringing, the boyfriend in turn told the school counselor, who in turn called the authorities. When the report reached law enforcement, a police car was sent to the school to pick up this young woman—in front of all her peers—and she was taken to the police station, where she

113

was interviewed by a detective, who at first seemed compassionate. Her parents were called in and interviewed separately, only to deny all the allegations and make their daughter look like a liar. The detective returned from the interview with the parents and struck a completely different tone with her. He then informed her that because she had consenting sex with her same-age boyfriend, that both would be charged for having sex as minors and for smoking pot, if she persisted with her story about her father molesting her. Law enforcement explained they were at a loss because they could neither prove her allegations were true nor that the father was innocent. They recommended the father move out for a brief time and the family follow up with family counseling. Unfortunately, this young woman ended up being lumped into a group of acting-out teens, who had ongoing drug issues and behavioral problems and nothing regarding the sexual abuse was ever addressed nor treated.

She remembers coming home and having the whole family treat her like she was a bad person, but strangely enough, her father packed his bags and stayed with some family members for a while. Her mother, who had her own sexual abuse history as a child, dismissed her story completely, and argued that there was no way things happened as early as she had alleged, because "as a child she did not even have breasts, at that time." To this day, the father denies any recollection of ever having done anything sexually inappropriate to his daughter, and he uses his severe alcoholism and his drug abuse at the time as his way of removing any kind of responsibility. Sounds familiar, doesn't it?

Nevertheless, his daughter ended up with a long list of symptoms caused by the sexual abuse, which include that she still feels that sleep is dangerous, she is terrified of the dark, she had to deal with nightmares for as long as she can think, and she tried to stay up as long as she could so that she would not have to wake up to another assault on her body and her psyche. She dealt with years and years of insomnia, body dysmorphia, panic attacks, and severe depression with ongoing suicidal ideations. The main thought in the back of her mind for all those encounters was, *I don't want to be here anymore*, which she is still working on. Again, I feel that it is a miracle that she is still here, and able to tell her story.

REFLECTIONS

It is gut-wrenching for me to hear about the way her situation was handled, especially by the authorities, and it confirms over and over that those victims who do not want to follow through with reporting their abuse have a rather solid reason for not doing so. Just being pulled out of school in front of your peers and having them watch you being put in the back of a cop car and taken away is traumatizing enough. Having to tell your whole story to complete strangers, without having any warning or having any advocate present, is terrifying enough. But having every detail turned upside down and used against you, and having your abuser sit in the other room, getting away with murder, is just about as bad as it gets.

Her boyfriend acted in good faith, and he was trying to protect his girlfriend who had disclosed to him what she had to endure for most of her upbringing. He had always been very respectful and never assaulted her, unlike what her own father had done to her for years. It saddens me to share that her school counselor, who made the mandatory report, never followed up with her, which made this young woman not only feel unimportant, but she felt she obviously didn't even deserve the school's support, either. Law enforcement knew there had to be something to her claim, because they asked her father to leave the home for a while—which he did—and they recommended that the family receive family counseling, which was at least a step in the right direction.

Unfortunately, there was no follow up or oversight, and the family enrolled the young woman into a counseling program for delinquent teens. She ended up being grouped with teens who had gotten into trouble with the law and who were addicted to drugs and alcohol, which had nothing to do with her situation, considering she had smoked marijuana perhaps twice in her life. The family session consisted of focusing on her delinquent behavior and how her parents needed to handle her, but nobody ever mentioned the reason why the family was ordered to seek counseling, meaning the topic of sexual abuse was never brought up or addressed in any shape or form.

115

NARRATIVE # 7

THIS YOUNG MAN DOES NOT remember much prior to his original trauma, other than that he grew up in a good family with Mom and Dad and his identical twin. When he was in second grade, his family relocated, and he and his brother were adjusting to their new school and their new surroundings. Something unusual was happening when the young man, then eight years old, began having issues with bed wetting, which he did not have prior to the move. The family tried all sorts of aids to see if they could deal with the issue by themselves, but when none of them worked, it became clear to the parents that they needed to consult with an MD.

The parents made an appointment with a urologist, and while they were all in the doctor's office, the urologist happened to have a glucometer at hand and decided to check the boy's blood sugar. The meter was not able to give an accurate reading, but it alerted the doctor that the blood sugar was extremely high. The MD sent the family immediately to the nearest Emergency Room where the young boy was diagnosed with type-1 diabetes, at eight years old. He was immediately admitted and after a few days, transferred to the children's hospital in the area, where he received more intense treatment.

The life of this young boy was changed overnight. While in the hospital, where his blood was taken every hour, he remembers crying and pleading with the staff to please stop sticking him with needles all the time. At the time of his diagnosis, insulin was in its infancy, and the treatment was most often thought of as coming in the form of food restrictions: no sugar, no ice cream, and no candy, period. At school he had to report to the nurse's station, and he had to have snacks every two hours. Emotionally, he does not remember anything other than that he thinks that he checked out because of his diagnosis and the fact that everything in his life from that point on changed so significantly. He remembers his mom giving him his shots for about two years, and then he took over giving himself his injections at the age of ten or eleven. He was sent to two different camps for kids with type-1 diabetes to help him deal with the emotional aspects of his diagnosis. Again, he has rather vague memories of being there, and he cannot access or verbalize how he was impacted emotionally.

Four years later, his identical twin brother was also diagnosed with type-1 diabetes, and he can only imagine how that must have impacted his brother, who had watched him go through four very difficult and painful years. Unfortunately, he cannot ask his brother about that because sadly, his brother took his own life at the age of thirteen. He happened to be the one home alone with his brother, and he was the one who found his brother with a gunshot wound to his head. He remembers trying to protect the rest of the family when they returned home, as far as dealing with that horrific site. His brother was dealing with a few life stressors at the time, but the young man is convinced that the medical diagnosis was a main contributor to his brother's decision to take his own life. He cannot recall how he emotionally dealt with the tragic loss of his brother at the age thirteen either, because everything from then on is very much a blur. All he knows for sure is that he shut down completely after that.

His teenage years were clearly overshadowed with grief and loss, and apparently, he displayed such a marked change in behavior that his family became concerned. He recalls that he stopped going to school eventually, and his parents sent him to a mental-health treatment facility for youth for quite some time because they did not want to lose him in the same way they lost his brother. His PTSD went basically untreated for many, many years until he was finally able to approach the topic and is still dealing with it.

He states that he had to deal with depression and anxiety ever since he was diagnosed with type-1 diabetes, and he struggled with his own suicidality off and on. Later in life, he made one attempt which he was able to abort at the last minute, and fortunately it did not claim his life. He feels that what led him to consider such a devastating move was partly due to his medical diagnosis and the life-long struggles that come with it, and partly a serious argument he had which might have triggered some memories of his brother and himself.

REFLECTIONS

Siblings of the individual who committed suicide have been called the forgotten bereaved, and the number of siblings that have lost a brother or sister to suicide is bigger than we would want to believe. It is not unusual for the surviving sibling to develop symptoms including depression, anxiety, lack of energy, disrupted-sleep patterns, difficulty concentrating, feelings of guilt, social withdrawal, and even suicidality. Often the feelings of shock and numbness are followed by feelings of anger, sadness, and vulnerability, perhaps longer than any other loss, due to the self-inflicted nature of the loss. Many have likened the unexpectedness of the suicide as if they had been hit by lightning and the traumatic loss challenged their own assumptions of their existence in the world. Not only did the loss make great demands on their capacity to deal with what had happened, but they also felt that they were , after all, "only the sibling," and it was their parents who were suffering the greatest loss. Siblings generally hesitate to lean on their parents for support in their bereavement, because if they see their parents being sad, they do not want to add to their parent's burden, and if they see their parents in a better mood, they do not want to draw attention to their loss. So, many try to avoid about talking about the suicide and instead, they choose to withdraw, which only gets them more attention, because the parents might panic when they see that the surviving sibling displays behaviors that they think might have led up to the suicide of their other child (Dyregrov & Dyregrov, 2005).

What started as a medical emergency at first, unfortunately, turned into a serious loss due to a tragic suicide. Having been diagnosed with type-1 diabetes as early as eight years old is one thing, but losing a loved one because of the disease is really another. It is a well-known fact that a medical condition such as type-1 diabetes has significant effects on someone's psyche and some serious effects on one's emotional terrain, just by itself. It is not unusual to feel run down, overwhelmed, and emotionally drained having to deal with the constant tracking of blood-sugar levels, the dosing of insulin, and the constant worry about your meals. Anger is such an important part of the journey toward acceptance of the disease, as much as denial and a hope for a cure are. While anger is a natural response, not too many people around us are comfortable dealing with it, and many of us have to learn how to channel our anger in ways that do not cause harm to anyone including ourselves and/or hurt any of our relationships.

With the diagnoses of diabetes, depression will sneak in no matter what, and it is not unusual for patients to not only become hopeless, but also deal with serious issues of suicidality. He recently had the opportunity to speak to a young man who was newly diagnosed with type-1 diabetes, struggling with the adjustment to his new and restrictive life, and already on an insulin pump only two years into the disease. The young man questioned if he had ever contemplated suicide, and he responded by saying, "Yes ... but no matter how bad you feel, consider that the impact of a suicide on a family is unimaginably painful and has very long-term effects on those left behind." He shared with this young man that he is grateful he was able to begin his recovery from his complex trauma and can finally make sense of what he has been dealing with.

NARRATIVE # 8

THIS YOUNG WOMAN DOES NOT remember anything being significantly wrong in her home until she was about four years old. One day she realized that her older sibling, who was chasing her through the house, was intending to seriously harm her, and that she was in real danger of getting hurt. That marked the beginning of her physical abuse until she was about fifteen years old. Needless to say, as she got older, the abuse got worse and worse. The parents did not intervene other than scolding the older brother every once in a while if the abuse happened directly in front of their eyes. Little did they know that the abuse became even worse outside the home, on the way to school and back, where the beatings were so intense they left black eyes, bloody noses, and bruises which left her in incredible pain and should have been extremely alarming to anyone around. The physical abuse by her sibling, combined with the emotional neglect and lack of protection from her caregivers, certainly set the tone for what happened next.

She describes her father as the provider who was always working—even on weekends—who was never home and was always emotionally unavailable, and she describes her mother as mentally unstable, overly dramatic, off the charts emotionally, and as someone who needed to be always out and about. Because both parents were frequently out of the house, they arranged for full-time nannies, and she remembers a lot of turnover. One time, they hired a male nanny, a young man who was an alcoholic and drunk by about noon every day. In the beginning, the young man would place her in his lap and make her move up and down, which seemed like play at first, but developed quickly into inappropriate touch. She still remembers that things quickly evolved into sexual abuse and that as she would zone out when things became too much for her to handle, she would freeze and focus on the cartoons that were running in the background on the TV and that this went on for a long time.

Her saving grace was not that she could talk to her parents or that the ongoing sexual abuse was discovered, but that the male nanny was fired because he was found drunk and completely passed out in the backyard, when her mom came home early one day, and she happened to discover him.

She recalls being in fourth grade and in charge of making lunches for her brother and herself every day. And if she forgot, her brother would take her behind some bushes on the way home and she would get a serious beating for that. She tried to get away from him whenever possible, and at one point tried to outsmart him by taking an earlier bus than him, which only worked for a little while until he caught on and quickly rearranged his schedule to be on the same bus as her again. On the way home, it was her job to dash to the bus station and convince the bus driver to wait for her brother, who did not feel that he needed to hurry and if she did not make it there in time, he would say, "Okay, let's walk," which let her know what to expect next. Again, she would get a severe beating, which usually left her with a bloody nose and in excruciating pain. She recalls that she had about two minutes flat to make it from her school to the bus stop. One time, she was so terrified of a beating, that she ran across the busy intersection and practically threw herself in front of the bus, so the bus driver had to make an emergency stop—and she pleaded for the driver to wait for the brother. One would think that someone would catch on to what was happening, but unfortunately, nobody did.

Over the years, her mother had two more babies, which her dad was furious about, and eventually the two divorced. It did not take long, and her mother connected with another man, who ended up moving in with her and her three siblings, and a blended family was born. After some financial issues, the family lost all their assets, including the home that her mother was able to keep in the divorce. First, they ended up in some questionable, rat-infested apartment, and finally they all had to move into a single motel room. To get away from all the drama, at age fifteen, she started volunteering at a nearby hospital. Against all odds, she was hired at the age of seventeen, because she graduated from high school early and demonstrated her work ethic. She applied for her own apartment and managed to work every possible shift available to save up enough money for a security deposit and three months' rent up front, since she didn't have any credit—still being under eighteen. By the time she was done paying for all the deposits, first month's rent, and utilities, she was left with pennies to pay for a mattress cover because she couldn't afford a mattress or bedding and ended up sleeping on the floor, using her clothing as a blanket.

While this young woman started her own life, her mother had four more children with the second husband, and eventually went overseas with him and all her children to take care of his elderly parents. Slowly but surely, the calls came in from her two younger siblings from the first marriage, stating that they were miserable and wanted to come back home. Her older brother by then was diagnosed with chronic mental-health issues and admitted to a residential mental-health treatment facility. The calls from her two younger siblings got more and more desperate, and after consulting with another family member overseas, she decided to go and rescue them. So, she booked a same-day round-trip airplane ticket for herself and two one-way tickets for her siblings. She met them at the airport and brought them back to the US. By then she was eighteen years old and had become a pseudo-parent of two. She enrolled the two in a private school and provided for them.

Several years later, she was notified by the same family member overseas that her mother was in trouble. The husband had her admitted to a psychiatric hospital where she resided for over six months, and she had no more will to live. So, this young woman decided to rescue her mom as well, and she pleaded with the husband to arrange for her mom to be discharged and flown back to the US where she could take care of her. The husband and the hospital staff agreed and discharged the mom, wheeling her mother straight to the airplane and home to the US. After years of putting her young life aside and solely providing for her whole family, her mother met another man, and decided to get remarried and move in with him with all her kids. Finally, the young woman got to focus on herself, which actually took some time to get used to.

REFLECTIONS

Sibling physical aggression is more prevalent than we would like to believe, and our societal awareness of sibling abuse has unfortunately lagged far behind other forms of child abuse. It is generally not only underreported, but it also receives little attention, partly because It is very difficult to assess within the ongoing family dynamics. The family configurations that are commonly found in sibling abuse are families where protective factors are absent, such as a parent who provides oversight, accountability, and a way to correct abusive behaviors. The absence of a parent figure often creates a structure in which older siblings generally have more accessibility to their younger and more vulnerable siblings and where there is an increased opportunity for the abuse to occur and go undetected. So, when the parents in this narrative returned to the home, not only would they never see any evidence of her injuries, but she would also not report the abuse for fear that there was no protection from her abuser and that the sibling would take things out on her even worse than he already did.

Since both parents were absent from the home and the babysitters not only had quite a turnover but were struggling with addiction and eventually included a sexual predator, there was no adequate parental oversight or protection. Therefore, this young woman was officially in charge of chores that should not have been hers to begin with, such as making the lunches for the older sibling, or for both of them to get to and from school on time—a chore that was assigned to her by the older sibling. The brutal beatings went unnoticed because her older sibling forced her to put her school clothing in the wash daily to remove all the blood stains to erase any evidence of the terrible beatings she received. Though she was in severe pain pretty much every day of that part of her life, she did not dare to show her injuries or complain about her pain for fear of retaliation.

Over time, this young woman became the pseudo-parent that her younger siblings learned to rely on heavily. Since siblings constitute an ongoing sense of family, there is often a deep-seated sense of obligation and responsibility to provide for them, as we can see very clearly in this narrative. Because of that, this young woman raised two younger siblings as soon as she became of age and eventually, she became the sole provider for her whole family, including her mother. Because her mother's second marriage failed and because of her poor mental health, she relied on this young woman to be able to come back to the United States. The mother was completely unable to provide for herself or for the rest of her family for many years, which placed a huge burden on this young woman and significantly delayed her own personal development in her early adulthood, and in particular delayed her post-traumatic growth. Again, siblings who grew up in an environment where children are deprived of parental care, authority, and control, not only have more access to each other which creates opportunities for sibling abuse, but it also creates an environment in which siblings create rather deep ties to each other and where the younger siblings look to their older siblings for pseudo-parental support, which is exactly what happened in this narrative.

NARRATIVE # 9

THIS YOUNG WOMAN WAS BORN to her teenage mother and a father who she never met, because shortly after her birth he ended up in prison. When the man was released, he never cared to find out about his little girl, and instead he decided to create a new life with another woman, which she recently gathered from social media. While the man is still in and out of jail and or prison to this day, she did learn that she has some half brothers and sisters, which is causing her great distress because she most likely will never get to know them, and she most likely will never be able to protect them.

Her mom had her own adverse childhood experiences, and her grandmother and her great-grandmother all share the same history. When her mother became pregnant with her at a very young age, both grandmother and great-grandmother jumped in to support mother and child, trying to avoid a negative outcome for them. They provided for mother and daughter until her mom got on her own feet, fell in love with another man, and moved away from the family of origin. Her mom wanted to make a life for herself and she was hoping for a great outcome for her and her newly created blended family.

The young woman remembers how happy she was to have a real father figure in her life, and for a short season, life seemed better than it had ever been. It did not take too long, and the dream fell apart. Not only did domestic violence develop, but the violence was accompanied by severe alcohol abuse and everything went downhill from there, very quickly. She became a witness to increasing physical and emotional abuse by her new father figure toward her mom, at a young age, but she also became the protector of the little son that had been born into the chaos. The violent outburst were usually followed by her mom's severe bouts of depression, which included severe suicidal ideations at the time. The young girl became extremely worried about her mom's well being, and she decided to become the protector and caretaker of her small sibling as best she could. She took over diaper changes, feedings, and soothing the baby when mom was not feeling well.

As if these toxic stressors were not enough, the stepparent eventually began sexually abusing this young girl, which continued undetected for several years. Finally, child protective services and law enforcement became involved, she was removed from the home, and lived with her grandparents for a good number of years. But, because she had developed a strong sense of responsibility for her younger sibling, and because she had such a strong and loving bond with her mom, it made it very difficult for her to have to leave the home, even after the sexual abuse was discovered.

As she got older, and because she missed her mom and her siblings so badly, she asked to spend time at her mom's home and to stay overnight, years after she had been removed from the home. The request seemed reasonable at the time, because she was older and had grown into her teenage years, and because everybody thought the issues had been resolved.

Being at her mom's house and being older, made her see things in a different light. She noticed that every time her mom tried to stay sober, it was the stepparent who would provide her with more alcohol as quickly as he could, enabling her heavy drinking. And if mom became severely depressed and suicidal, it was the stepparent who encouraged her and provided the means for her to be able to follow through with her plan. She further noticed that her mom was completely cut off from the outside world—not only had mom lost her driver's license, but she had absolutely no transportation, she had no access to money, and she was basically trapped in her own home. The stepparent, who supposedly had no recollection of ever being inappropriate with the young woman and who blamed his "blackouts" for his inappropriate actions in the past, began sexually assaulting her just like he had before, when she happened to stay the night.

When she entered trauma therapy, new reports were made to the authorities, and legal procedures and charges were put into motion. Though the abuser was held responsible for his sexual abuse of a minor in court, to this day he has to acknowledge that his actions were criminal, and he is still hiding behind his supposed alcohol black-outs. When her mom realized what was happening to her daughter when she was staying at her home, she fought even harder for her sobriety, because she knew her daughter would not fabricate such allegations. When the young woman became brave enough to talk about these sexually inappropriate incidents with her mom, her mom listened and she did not dismiss but instead validated her horrible experiences. Mom was able to sustain her sobriety and she decided to leave the toxic relationship, so she could be with her children and they could live a life without abuse and begin their recovery.

REFLECTIONS

It was not until her mother became strong enough to remove herself from the abuse, and it was not until mother, daughter, and the younger sibling were safely reunited, that the young woman was willing to move forward in her trauma recovery. Having her family back was a huge milestone, while the charges regarding the sexual abuse kept hanging over her head. The young woman did not know from one day to the next if she would have to appear in a court of law, or if she would have to face her abuser and divulge every single detail in public.

Eventually she found her own voice and she was able to face her abuser in court. She put together a witness statement that did not leave any doubt to what had happened to her as well as the fact that she was very much on the way to recovery, She made it very clear that had it not been for the serious concerns for her mom and little sibling, she likely would have never asked to return to the family home. She let the abuser know that she had absolutely no idea the sexual abuse would ever happen again, especially after she had been removed from the home with the help of Child Protective Services and after living with other family members for years. What mattered most to her was that her mom and her sibling were in a terribly abusive situation and they needed support—and there was no way she would have ever left them behind.

Eventually, this young woman saw her mom address her own complex trauma issues and she was able to witness her mom fight her addiction issues and succeed. Not only did her mom choose her over the perpetrator, which was extremely important to this young woman, but she also saw her mom for the first time in her life, work on her own trauma issues and begin to live a much healthier life. With her family being safe she was able to continue her own healing journey and work towards restoring some levels of her innocence. Her goal is not to have to live out and hand on the painful generational patterns, which all the other females in her lineage were burdened with.

PART 4

CHAPTER 14

THE JOURNEY TO AND FROM THE UNDERWORLD

LET ME GIVE YOU A Depth Psychological perspective on the healing journey of complex trauma survivors and share with you the Egyptian myth of Innanna, who was the Queen of Heaven and decided one day to travel to meet her sister, Ereshkigal, the Queen of the Underworld. Ereshkigal's husband Gugalana had died, and reportedly the queen was absolutely inconsolable in her grief. Innanna wanted to comfort her sister and she made conscious preparations for her journey, which included telling her faithful servant Ninshubur how to seek help for her among the gods in case she did not return within three days. Nobody was in favor of her dangerous undertaking, including the gods, but Innanna insisted on going on to console her sister, no matter what.

When Innanna came to the gates of the underworld, she announced her arrival with a fierce cry and a loud knock. Ereshkigal's chief gatekeeper answered the door and delivered Innanna's message to the queen. It was decided that Innanna would be granted entrance, and that she would have to pass through the seven gates to the underworld. With that she would be stripped and bowed low. When Innanna entered the throne room, her grief-stricken sister Ereshkigal arose and had the judges of the underworld surround her, who passed judgment on Inanna and decided to fasten the eye of death onto her. Innanna turned into a rotting corpse, hanging on a metal peg.

After three days and three nights, when Innanna did not return as promised, her faithful servant sought help from the gods. Most of them were angry with Innanna for her dangerous journey, but Father Enki, who was most troubled and grieved by Innanna's fate, granted the request for help. He molded two tiny creatures from the dirt beneath his fingernails, breathed life into them, and off they went—able to slip into the underworld unnoticed, where they began to assist the Queen of the Underworld. Ereshkigal was groaning and moaning, stricken by grief over the loss of her husband and dealing with her symbolic labor pains when they arrived. They continued to serve her and eventually, Ereshkigal was able to transform her grief and gave birth to her renewed self as well as to the renewed self of Innanna.

When Ereshkigal finally stopped moaning, she was filled with such gratitude that she wanted to reward those two little creatures who had served her so empathically, and she asked them what they desired as a gift. They requested Innanna's corpse, which was granted to them. With the food and water of life given to them by Father Enki, they revived Innanna's body, and she eventually arose. As Innanna was preparing for her ascent, the demons of the underworld clung to her and informed her that no one leaves the underworld unmarked, and that for her to return, someone needed to take her place.

Upon her return, Innanna threw herself at her faithful servant's feet. The demons requested Ninshubur take her place, but Innanna refused and argued that Ninshubur was her right arm and had saved her life. So, the demons prepared to take Umma in Innanna's place, who had come to look for his mother, and Innanna argued that her son was her left arm, and again she refused for him to be taken. Finally, Innanna fastened the eye of death on her husband Dumuzi, who had not been bothered by his wife's absence, and who had remained dressed in his shiny garments on his shiny throne. So Innanna chose for him to be taken to the underworld in her place. Though Innanna encountered madness in the underworld, it enabled her to become the goddess of both realms, the realm of the day and the realm of the night. By consciously accepting her journey,

132

she was able to unite the mysteries of light and dark and transform humiliation into humility.

I have yet to meet a complex trauma survivor who does not relate to the metaphor of having their rotting corpse hanging on a metal peg, especially in the very beginning of their healing journey. I do not think I could describe the feeling of being in the midst of severe depression, anxiety, and complete devastation for such an extended period of our life in any better way. Too often have we survivors ventured out to comfort or be comforted, only to be stripped of absolutely everything. At times it very much feels as if we literally had the sign of death fastened to our forehead. The concept of making conscious provisions for our journey, I believe, is rather foreign to us, especially since most of us do not have a loyal servant or a trusted family member who we can completely count on, and who would be willing and able to plead with the gods in our behalf, in case we are unable to return. While the process of overwhelming grief and being completely inconsolable is pretty very familiar to us, the eventual transformation that occurs after suffering so severely is something we have most likely never experienced before.

One of the parts of the myth I like to point out is that because of our journey into the underworld, into the grief and losses we have experienced for most of our lifetime, it does eventually become clear to most of us that our healing journey—or even the smallest parts of it—will never be in vain. When we come to a place where we are ready to let go of some of our worst pain and we are able to allow it to somehow transform us, even to a small degree, we become more able to be in the light as well as the darkness, simultaneously. With that we no longer have to live in the world of the extremes, which I find one of the most freeing aspects of undertaking such a difficult and, at times, life-threatening journey.

The statement, "nobody leaves the underworld unmarked," is a given, but the concept that for us to be able to ascend, someone has to take our place in the underworld was something I could not relate to at first. Too many of the perpetrators sat on their lofty thrones, in their shiny garments, denying any type of responsibility, thinking that they did not need to bother or get involved in any part of our painful journey. But if I look at the many narratives I have been able to witness, I saw some perpetrators who were found guilty of their heinous acts and who had to serve a well-deserved sentence—then that exchange makes more sense to me.

Like many other complex trauma survivors, I needed some type of roadmap, something that would help me better understand where I was in my healing journey, and I would like to share some of the tools that I have found extremely helpful. They helped me to measure the progress I had already made, or the type of personal growth which I needed to focus my attention on, as I was clawing my way out of my cave, metaphorically speaking. The first tool is the Post-Traumatic Stress Disorder or PTSD Growth Inventory by Tedeschi & Calhoun, and the second tool is the Connor-Davidson Resilience Scale. These tools are helpful, because not knowing where we are at any given time in our journey, increases our levels of anxiety and depression, which does not make us feel any safer in a world which does not seem terribly "safe" to us to begin with.

The PTSD Growth Inventory focuses on five main areas, or better, it measures five factors with twenty-one items including: relating to others, new possibilities, personal strength, spiritual changes, and appreciation of life. The full Connor Davidson Resilience scale has twenty-five items, and the brief Connor Davidson Resilience Scale has ten items, and their original design measured factors such as: personal competency, standards and tenacity, trust in one's instincts, tolerance of negative effects of stress, and positive acceptance of change, to name a few major ones. I use the scales as a guideline throughout the treatment of individuals in the third phase of their recovery, when the focus is basically on reintegration into the rest of society.

Resiliency is usually not looked upon as a single construct, but it is conceptualized to be composed of a number of different components, which all of us possess to a greater or lesser degree. The eight core components which are outlined in the psi Resilience Questionnaire are as follows:

- an individual's level of confidence to address problems and difficulties;
- the extent that an individual believes that there can be good outcomes in life and that one can recover from setbacks;
- an individual's clear goals and the commitment to attain those goals;
- the extent an individual is able to adapt to changing circumstances;
- the extent of an individual's perception to change their behavior and their response to changing circumstances;
- the extent to which an individual can deal with challenging circumstances and can perceive challenges as an opportunity for growth;
- the extent to which an individual can remain calm in the face of a stressor and control his or her emotions;
- the extent to which an individual is able to ask for help and accept support.

These components of resiliency are usually deployed when we face increased pressure, challenges, setbacks, or changes. In order for us to use the most beneficial strategy, though, it is helpful to know where we are in the *Thrive Cycle of Resilience*, which helps us understand if we are in the survival, adaptation, recovery, or thrive stage. I believe it would help support systems to understand these concepts as well, because it can explain how we might be able to respond, how we might be able to adjust to changes, how we might be able to bounce back from adversity, and how we might be able to grow from facing adversities.

I want to give you a life example of how our resiliency and our ability to adjust to stress can develop once we have been able to work through some of our trauma. Let me go back about a decade or so, when I had been working at the hospital for a number of years. Some staff began asking me occasionally if I was always "looking for the pony," no matter what I was dealing with. I honestly had no idea what they were referring to, because English is my second language, until one of them explained to me the saying was based on a story of a child finding a pile of manure under the Christmas Tree. Instead of being disappointed, he began to shovel because he was convinced that "with that much manure, there had to be a pony underneath it, somewhere." That was a great illustration as to how I was and am dealing with the stress of my work, especially when on the frontline, and I was able to answer these questions from then on with a firm YES. I do not run away from a seemingly hopeless situation, and I literally start shoveling, because I am determined to look for any small positive aspect in any type of crisis, no matter how bad things seem on the outside. I am always looking for any type of lesson that can be learned, without dismissing its severity or minimizing any suffering, because that is literally how I got to where I am today, personally and professionally.

I firmly believe, that as much as we all need true compassion when we are facing any crisis and we are suffering deep emotional pain, we can all use that small synchronistic event or that one person that can somehow help us make some type of sense of things, of course, in a very gentle and loving way. Suffering without any type of purpose seems so incredibly pointless, which makes an awful lot of sense to me (Frankle, 1988).

Trust me, it is difficult for us to initially imagine that we will get to a place in our healing journey where we will gain more insight into what happened to us and will actually begin to understand more and more how our long-term consequences are still affecting our life, unfortunately, most of the time in rather negative ways. And that we will gain the tools needed to deal with any type of negative life events or any unexpected triggers more effectively. And that in the process, we will most likely learn that not all life stressors have to turn into another crisis, or must have a bad outcome. And that over time, we will even learn that we are a lot stronger than we think we are, and that the person we will be able to trust the most will one day be ourselves. Please understand, these things do not happen overnight, and for a moment, things may even seem to get worse as we venture out and try to face our original trauma as well as our long-term consequences. It takes a lot of courage to unwrap our trauma history and face things head on, without using the behaviors we developed to either comfort ourselves or dissociate ourselves from these ugly memories. I can only reiterate that we can use all the compassion, encouragement, and support we can get while we are on our rather challenging journey to and from the underworld.

Though we have grown in a number of areas of our lives it does not mean we cannot experience deep distress from time to time. And though we have made some progress as far as our posttraumatic growth is concerned, that does not mean we no longer have some form of PTSD. In general, it means we have gained some tools to deal with serious stressors more effectively, we are more likely to recover more quickly, and we may not necessarily have to relive our original trauma when we get triggered unexpectedly. Once we have been able to establish basic safety and stability in our lives, and once we have been able to work through our intrusive memories and make sense of our "crazy" narrative, we usually come to a place where we can work toward the integration of our fragmented parts of self and our reintegration into society.

As professionals we need to be able to sit with the individual who is in deep emotional pain, postpone any type of judgment, and make sure we do not do any harm or make the person feel any worse about themselves than they already do. I believe that any support system, any professional, and any bystander would make our journey a lot less complicated if they had the tools to do some of the same, so that together we may make a difference, and together we may make this world a better and safer place overall.

CHAPTER 15

COMPASSION AND SELF-COMPASSION

AS ADULT SURVIVORS OF ADVERSE childhood experiences, we often carry our heavy burden for life, and generally, we do not expect any of it to be carried by anyone else. Yet we long for compassion, hope for understanding, and ache for any bit of support, which by the way, does not require any specialized training. When we finally get to a place where we can wrap our heads around what happened to us during our developmental years and when we begin to understand the long-term effects of our trauma, we often find ourselves rather overwhelmed by the complexity of it all. At that point, what we need the most from the people around us is understanding that we are just at the beginning of our recovery journey, and we have been most likely navigating the best we could, with all of our limitations and imperfections. Truth is, we lived in a different universe with very different rules and expectations, with blurred boundaries and severe punishment, which by the way, were never consistent and ever changing. Many of us lived in isolation, and the only life skill we were able to truly develop was our ability to survive. What we were not able to develop was the ability to connect with others. Therefore, it should not come as a surprise that we have difficulty dealing with our post-trauma world, which we hardly understand, nor have we ever been prepared for.

In my experience, the way to overcome the gap that exists between survivors and non-survivors is learning to be compassionate with each other. Because true compassion is neither an act of

139

rescuing nor is it an act of pity, but it is based on an understanding that the other person is indeed suffering, and all we can offer is a willingness to make a human connection in the face of that suffering. It means that we allow the person who is in pain to sit with their pain in the absence of judgment, discomfort, terror, or fear.

> Compassion is fueled by understanding and accepting that we are all made of strength and struggle—[and the fact] that no one is immune to pain or suffering; [therefore] compassion is not a practice of [being] better than, or an attitude of "I can fix you"—but [instead] it's a practice based in the beauty and pain shared by humanity (Brenee` Brown, 2021, p.116).

From the vantage point of a complex trauma survivor who is trying to regain his or her composure in the face of an often-unexpected trigger, the act of quietly sitting, perhaps in the presence of a complete stranger, is really the only hands-on support needed. The rest of the complex issues need to be addressed and dealt with at some other time, in the most appropriate recovery setting available. Yet, this quiet moment of sitting and showing kindness and compassion, this moment of human connection, often gives us survivors the courage to continue on our difficult recovery journey, because it reaffirms that somebody, even if it is a total stranger, seriously cares.

If compassion is an emotional response to us feeling empathy and creates a desire in people to help, and empathy is our awareness of another person's emotions and an attempt to understand how the other person may be feeling, then we need to examine more closely how they both impact survivors of complex trauma. Many people believe that demonstrating empathy means "walking in another person's shoes" to acquire true understanding, but empathy actually means truly listening to another person's narrative and believing what they are saying, even when their story doesn't match our own experience (Brown, 2021).

Since survivors of complex trauma have lived through unthinkable and heinous acts of physical, emotional, and sexual violence, it is often very difficult for others to imagine that what we are talking about actually happened. I believe it is incredibly important to realize that not believing us or arguing with us and dismissing what we are sharing in that moment may result in retraumatization, however intentional or unintentional. Simply put, believe us when we tell our stories, because rest assured, true trauma survivors do not want to make up heinous acts or abuse to get attention or create stories just for the fun of it. We do not need sympathy, and the last thing we need is pity, because these sentiments, again, only set us apart from the rest of the world and reinforce the "otherness" we have already experienced for most of our lives. Furthermore, being on the receiving end of sympathy or pity feels both cold and isolating and leaves us feeling even more vulnerable. Therefore, it is extremely important to remember our shared humanity, and that in spite of the fact that we have experienced the unthinkable and unimaginable, we are not that different from people who have not experienced complex trauma. In short, the best sentiment a non-survivor—whether a friend, a co-worker, or a professional—can offer us is human connection, sitting with us in our suffering, believing the narratives we share, and empathizing with us.

On top of what we have experienced in the past, the truth is, its impact will not just dissolve or disappear, only because our original trauma has finally subsided. Since we have been inundated with horribly negative messages and awful labels about ourselves, it may not come as a surprise that most of us have internalized them, and they have become a crucial part of our ongoing self-talk. So even if our original trauma is in the past, that negative self-talk and our negative core beliefs have taken over our internal landscape. That includes constant questions and ideas which suggest that we have to be bad people, because why else would anybody in their right mind treat a child the way we were treated? Or, to counter that, if we were not bad to begin with, having lived through and suffered unspeakable torture and abuse, by now we certainly must be too broken and too damaged; therefore, we surely must have become bad people. On top of that we often question, even as adults, if perhaps we could have prevented the abuse, or if, as we were told so many times, perhaps we did ask for such horrific treatment. We have a hard time understanding why on earth, any human being would treat another human being like our abusers treated us.

When I share the kind of thoughts that used to hijack my brain for decades with other survivors, they usually breathe a sigh of relief because they don't feel so alone anymore. They begin understanding that harmful inner monologue is a shared experience for most complex trauma survivors. This self-harming dialogue includes name calling, questioning every aspect of the self, undermining well-earned achievements, and becoming the single worst critic we'll ever face. When it comes to the latter, the inner critic's volume is on full blast in our minds, repeatedly saying things like:

- "Who do you think you are?"
- "What is wrong with you?"
- "Why can't you do anything right?"
- "There you go again, screwing up everything!"
- "You Idiot! You suck! See, you really are stupid!"
- "Nobody likes being around you!"
- "Everybody hates your guts!"
- "You are completely worthless!"
- "Nobody cares!"
- "Nobody will ever believe your story!"
- "Get over yourself!"
- "People will be so much better off without you!"

The litany of negative self-talk and accompanying internalized self-hatred is debilitating and directly related to our complex trauma, because we heard those horrible messages pretty much every day of our developmental years. Therefore, we ended up internalizing most of them because we did not know any better—we were so young. Not only did our abusers injure our mind, our body, and our soul at the moment of the abuse, but they made sure we would never believe we are actually deserving human beings, and think that nobody would ever believe us in case we would try to speak up at any time.

Developing that kind of recognition and seeing that our internal struggles with our inner critic are not only a unique experience but also very much a universal experience, eventually enables us to see that our negative core beliefs are a lasting byproduct of our abuse. Eventually that recognition makes it possible to develop self-compassion, which is one of the most important components of our healing journey, without which trauma recovery is nearly impossible.

It is extremely important to understand that our negative self-talk and our harsh internal critics are not so much the doing of the trauma survivor, but they are often a direct by-product of the unthinkable accusations our abusers leveled at us as children. From the standpoint of a child's underdeveloped brain, any abused child has simply no way of knowing if these types of horrific messages are actually true. Therefore, name calling, harsh judgment, and belittling self-talk develop internally and stay active well into our adulthood. While the adult complex trauma survivor may no longer intellectually recognize the internal messages as valid, emotionally the words are omnipresent and simply do not just disappear with age.

To silence the inner-critic and erase the childhood abuser's cruel words, there are four important aspects for self-compassion that we adult complex trauma survivors need to grasp. First, we have to learn and understand that we are part of humanity—even though we feel palpably separate from non-survivors—and that we are not as strange as we might think or have been made believe by others. The reality is that there are many complex trauma survivors who have been exposed to similarly cruel treatments, whose behaviors very much mirror our own. Second, we need to understand that our mistreatment was fundamentally inhumane and that our sometimes understandably flawed responses, including our negative self-talk, are nothing but human. Third, we need to learn to treat ourselves as we would treat others. Specifically, if we accept that every human being deserves kindness and compassion, we need to realize that we are worthy of it, too. Finally, we must learn that the benefits of mindfulness, especially maintaining an open-mind and postponing judgment, apply to us as much as they apply to "normal" people. In effect, we must learn to employ an attitude of loving kindness and compassion in the way we are dealing with ourselves, which is so utterly contrary to our inner monologue and core beliefs which have dominated our thoughts ever since our early childhood.

It is important for survivors and non-survivors alike to bear in mind that it takes time and serious work to undo our old mindset and to adopt even an ounce of mindfulness. Post-traumatic growth is not something that happens overnight or early in trauma recovery, but it usually occurs later in the healing journey. Oftentimes, it shows up first in the therapeutic setting, where we can safely move toward mindfulness and self-compassion. In fact, when my first psychologist mentioned that one of the goals in my treatment was for me to eventually become my own best friend, I was suddenly more concerned about his mental health than mine. The idea of even becoming an ally for myself seemed simply absurd, and it was as if he was speaking another language because his words were so unfamiliar to my post-trauma mind. It took many years of treatment for me to grasp the idea of self-love. It was a struggle for me to try to open-up my heart and mind to self-love while I was undertaking the broader emotional labor of my complex trauma recovery. My often ineffective behaviors and thoughts, including my negative self-talk, would want to take me right back to my all-too-familiar negative landscape, and many times I had to literally inch my way back. As a professional who understands how the post-trauma brain works, and who understands that my lived experience as a complex trauma survivor is consistent with that of many others, I can still find myself having to make a very conscious effort to apply mindfulness to myself.

It is believed that self-compassion helps make sense of our original trauma, and that self-compassion illuminates the way original trauma impacts our ability to regulate our emotions. While cognitively restructuring was helpful to me in the beginning of my treatment, it did not necessarily change my ability to regulate my emotions right away. When I could finally recognize, on a deeper psychological level, that I, too, was deserving of better treatment simply because I am part of humanity, it was a major turning point in my recovery. This turning point helped me move away from some of my harsh self-judgment and broader negative self-talk—both part of the fabric of my life since my early childhood. Much to my surprise, I began moving toward the ability of treating myself with more self-compassion.

Compassion emerges when love meets suffering, and mindfulness emerges when we become cognizant of the here and now and are no longer afraid of the present, moment-to-moment experiences. When we can get in touch with our emotional pain and are able to remain calm and non-reactive, that is actually what enables us to transform our painful experiences. Self-compassion is said to be a particular kind of acceptance that is fundamental to our capacity for true compassion itself. Equally important, self-compassion is a special awareness that can free us from the pain of childhood abuse by allowing us to accept the experience as our own (Germer & Neff, 2014).

Compassion and mindfulness allow us, therefore, to accept ourselves and our histories, and they enable us to appreciate that we, complex trauma survivors, are as deserving as the people around us. We see a new and present world in front of us, and when negative things happen, instead of engaging in our negative self-talk, we can now approach the present moment with questions like, "What just happened?" "How do I want to respond to that?" and "What do I really need right now?" instead.

As much as we complex trauma survivors strive for a sense of "normalcy" by quieting our harsh inner self-critic down and by learning and employing some levels of self-compassion, mindfulness in itself is a very challenging skill and/or attitude for us to develop. So in case we are harshly criticized, judged, or even put down—especially by people we may count on for our safety and well-being, such as our support system or even the legal system or the medical profession—we too often find ourselves vulnerable, triggered, and unexpectedly in fight-flight-freeze mode. The last thing we need in moments like that are harsh labels that mirror our abusers' messages, because fight-flight-freeze mode not only leads to self-criticism, self-isolation, and self-absorption, but it also causes us survivors to engage in old and unhealthy coping mechanisms. It can cause a lot of emotional harm and become tacitly retraumatizing.

As complex trauma survivors, we have to go moment-to-moment, but as we gain more insights and develop a language for our emotions and experiences, we eventually learn to better communicate with the people and professionals around us that may be supporting us in our new endeavors. Emotional safety is one of the most important elements of a supportive environment, and failing to engage with a complex trauma survivor with an attitude of compassion and mindfulness can easily lead to retrograde behaviors on the part of the survivor. While on the contrary, experiencing compassion and support in the face of reliving a horrible memory can help us to reprocess and reinterpret that memory and move us closer and closer to our recovery.

CONCLUSION

AS HUMAN BEINGS, WE ARE all exposed to a huge variety of lived experience and the summary of them creates the basis of how we understand, deal with, and approach our future experiences and what type of meaning we extrapolate from them in the world in which we are living. Though as human beings we have the unique ability to learn from the experience of others, we also know that human beings can be rather reluctant to do so for a number of different reasons. But we may have to remember, if it was simply a matter of access and opportunity for perpetrators to be able to disrupt our childhood so significantly or to harm us in any way later in life, then that would mean it could have been any of us who could have ended up with complex trauma.

Therefore, my hope for all of us is that we would be more prepared to respond in a more compassionate, open minded, and thoughtful way with anyone we come upon who is dealing with some type of trauma, no matter what the situation is. Most of the time we don't know why a person is finding him or herself in a vulnerable situation, or why a person might react seemingly irrational. In my opinion, unless that individual is causing any harm to anyone, including themselves, I believe we need to stay open minded and refrain from judgment, and give that person not only the benefit of the doubt, but also the space and support needed in that moment. I hope that with our increased knowledge and understanding of some of the difficult dynamics complex trauma survivors, in particular, might be dealing with, we might be better prepared to de-escalate any situation we come upon, instead of inadvertently escalating things.

Because I am keenly aware of the fact that lived experience can neither be categorized nor fully explained, I chose to use different human experiences to show the variety and possibilities of what it means to have survived complex trauma and have to deal with its long-term effects, perhaps for a lifetime. The topic has captured me partly because I have lived through it, but mainly because I have seen it play out for so many people in everyday life over and over again, and significantly interfere with the quality of their life and the overall level of their functioning, long after the original trauma was overcome. I have been and will continue to be passionate about capturing some of its essence as I have found myself in the role of survivor, healer, scholar, guardian, and defender, and I will do so for the rest of my life.

This phenomenological inquiry has been designed not only to increase understanding and insight, but to serve survivors and non-survivors alike, as a resource for situations they come across in everyday life. While there will neither be a great punchline, nor will there be a fancy summary at the end of this book, hopefully there will be a lot more understanding and open mindedness on the part of the reader. My hope is that it may help remove some of the stigma about mental health in general and specifically, the stigma so often assigned to those of us who suffer from complex trauma and are still struggling with some of the long-term effects. My hope is that it may also open doors for those who are willing to be of support and provide some hands-on tools as to what they could possibly do to help when they find themselves confronted by it. May this be yet another beginning of many more open and gentle discussions that do not have to end in terrible misunderstandings or unnecessary conflict.

Again, we are not asking for pity, and we are not asking for special treatment, but we are asking for compassion, understanding, and support, because dealing with the long-term effects is challenging, to say the least. We never know when we might be triggered, and it is even more disheartening for us when it happens in public and the spotlight shines directly upon us. Please don't ask us what is wrong with us or why we are still dealing with this or tell us to get our act together and to snap out of it in those moments. Instead, take time to listen, give us the benefit of the doubt, and if at all possible, give us a moment of privacy while we are trying to calm our internal landscape. Again, at that moment we may have difficulty articulating accurately what is going on with us, we may not feel safe in our surroundings to unfold our complete narrative, and we are most likely not even sure what internal alarms have been set off. I have yet to witness any complex trauma survivor who is offered time and space to regroup, not find that helpful or feel offended by that offer.

As you know, my goal is to educate, share, articulate, invite into, and shed light onto the complexity of this phenomenon. I have kept the description of our unique experiences as general as possible, giving just enough information to get the most important points across, and not traumatize or retraumatize anyone. I strove for precision and exactness as much as possible, using interpretive descriptions that exact the fullness and completeness of the phenomenon addressed in this book. I hope I was able to share what it means to experience life from a post-traumatic angle, so that non-survivors might be able to relate to us a bit more, and that I was able to communicate clearly how important and helpful it is for us to be met with a trauma-informed attitude by those around us.

It is my prayer that this work can help pave the way for someone to seek out trauma therapy and begin their own healing journey. If it can help a loved one, a family member, or a whole support team to better understand what their loved ones are going through, so the complex trauma survivors may be met with more empathy and compassion, it would be an amazing accomplishment. If it can be instrumental for someone not to take their own life, but to hang in there and not to give up, and come to the realization one day that life can be worth living after all, I will be truly humbled and extremely grateful.

I believe, together we have an even better chance to break the chains that have held us down for such a long time, and together we have a much better chance to beat the incredible odds, which have been stacked against us as survivors of complex trauma. If we can avoid at least some unnecessary retraumatization, such as dismissal, disbelief, and disrespect, we have a much better chance to heal and rewire our brain, so we do not have to live in our old, familiar universe anymore.

Perhaps, we would no longer have to feel like outsiders because of what happened to us at such an early age that changed the trajectory of our adult life so significantly. And perhaps it would allow us to be able to reconnect with the rest of society and make a smoother transition, coming out of the darkness and into the light.

REFERENCES

Bowins, Brad, Psychological defense Mechanisms, *The American Journal of Psychoanalysis*, Vol. 64, No. 1, March 2004

Brown, Brenee, 2021, The Atlas of the Heart, Random House

Burke-Harris, 2022, Understanding Adverse Childhood Experiences, Nadine Burke Harris: How childhood trauma affects health across a lifetime

Connor, Kathryn M., Assessment of Resilience in the Aftermath of Trauma, Physicians Postgraduate Inc. 2006; 67 (suppl 2)

Covington, Stephanie S., Women and Addiction: A Trauma Informed Approach, journal of Psychoactive Drugs, SARC Supplement 5, November 2008

Craparo, Giuseppe, The Role of Dissociation, Affect Dysregulation, and Developmental Trauma in Sexual Addiction; Clinical NeuroPsychiatry (2014) 11, 2, 86–90

Curtis, Christine A., Complex Trauma, Complex Reactions: Assessment and Treatment; Psychological Trauma: Theory, research, Practice and Policy, 2008, Vol, S, No. 1. 86–100

De Bellis, Michael D., Developmental traumatology: a contributory mechanism for alcohol and substance use disorders, Psychoneuroendocrinology 27 (2002) 155–170

Dyregrov, Kari and Dyregrov, Atle., Suicide and Life-Threatening Behaviors 35 (6), 2005, The American Association of Suicidology

Filitti, Vincent, The relation Between Adverse Childhood Experiences and Adult Health, *The Permanente Journal*, Winter 2002, Volume 6, No. 1, p. 44–47

Fisher, Janina, 2021, *Transforming the Living Legacy of Trauma*, PESI, Inc.

Frankle, Victor, 1988, Man Search for Meaning, Washington Square Press

Ford, Katherine; Barton, Emma: Newbury, Annamarie; Hughes, Karen; Bezeczky, Zoe; Roderick, Janine & Bellis, Mark, 2019, *The Prisoner ACE Survey*, Public Health Wales; Bangor University.

Germer, Christopher & Neff, Kristin, 2014, *The Mindful-Self-Compassion Workbook*, pp. 44–55

Greene, Carolyn A., Haisley, Lauren, Wallace, Cara, and Ford, Julian D., *Clinical Psychology Review*, Volume 80, August 2020, 101891

Herrman, Judith, 1997, Trauma and Recovery, Basic Books

Jackson-Nakazawa, Donna, 2015, *Disrupted Childhood*, Atria Paperback

Jung, Carl G., 1963, *Memories, Dreams, and Reflections*, Random House

Kalshed, Donald, 1996, *The Inner World of Trauma*, RoutledgeACE, CDC-Kaiser ACE study, 1995 -1997, Adverse Childhood Experiences

Kihlstrom, John F., The Trauma-Memory Argument, Consciousness and Cognition, 1995, 4, 63–67

Koetting, Cathy, , Trauma informed Care, Helping Patients with a Painful Past, Journal of Christian Nursing, 33 (4) p. 206 - 213

LaCapra, Dominick, TRAUMA, HISTORY, MEMORY, IDENTITY: WHAT REMAINS, History and Theory 55 (October 2016), 375–400

Lamphier, Gary, Traumatic Stress in Childhood can lead to brain changes in adulthood: study, Health and Wellness Research, February 2021

Liotti, Giovanni, Trauma Dissociation and Disorganized Attachment, *Psychotherapy: Theory, Research, Practice, Training*, 2004, Vol. 41, No. 4

Madigan, Lee and Gamble, Nancy, 1991, *The Second Rape*, Lexington Books

Mate', Gabor, Addiction: Childhood Trauma, Stress and the Biology of Addiction, Journal Compilation 2012, AARM, DOI 10.14200/jrm.2012.1.1005

Mate, Gabor, 2003, *When the Body says No*, Wiley

Mate', Gabor, 2012, The Power of Addiction and the Addiction to Power https://drgabormate.com

Mate', Gabor, 2019, The Myth of Normal in an Insanity Society. TEDxTalks, https://drgabormate.com

Matheson, Kimberly, Asokumar, Ajani, Anisman., Hymie; Resilience: Safety in the Aftermath of Traumatic Stressor Experience; Frontiers in Behavioral Neuroscience, 2020, 14: 596929

Moustafa, A., Parkes, D., Fitzgerald, L., Underhill, D., Garami, J., Levy-Gigi, E., Stramecki, Valikhani, Frydecka, D., Misiak, B., The Relationship between Childhood Trauma, Early Life-stress and Alcohol and Drug Use, Abuse, and Addiction: An Integrative Review, 2018, Current Psychology https://doi.org/10.1007/s12144-018-9973-9

Moustakas, Clark, 1994, *Phenomenological Research Methods*, Sage

Neff, Kristin and Germer, Christopher, 2018, *The Mindful Self-Compassion Workbook*, Guilford Press

Neubauer, Brain E., Witkop, Catherine T., Varpio, Lara; How Phenomenology can help us learn from the experiences of others, *Perspective on medical education*, Netherlands, 2019 April, Vol 8, No 2, p 90–97

Pimlott Kubiak, Sheryl, The Effects of PTSD on Treatment Adherence, Drug Relapse, and Criminal Recidivism in a Sample of Incarcerated Men and Women, Research on Social Work Practice (2004); 14; 424

Ramos, Catarina and Leal, Isabel; Post-Traumatic Growth in the Aftermath of Trauma: A Literature Review About related Factors and Application Contexts, Psychology & Community Health, 2013, Vol. 2 (1), 43–54, doi: 10.5964/psych. v2i1.39

Reber, Arthur S., 1995, *Dictionary of Psychology*, The Penguin

Ross, Colin A. and Halpern, Naomi, 2009, *Trauma Model Therapy*, Manitou

Ross, Colin A., 2013, *Structural Dissociation*, Manitou

van der Kolk, Bessel, Trauma and Memory, Psychiatry and Clinical Neuroscience, 2002, Vol, 52, Issue S1/p. S52–S64

Van der Kolk, Trauma and Memory, *Psychology and Clinical Neurosciences*, 2002, Vol. 52, Issue 51, p.S52–S64

Van der Kolk, Bessel, 2014, *The Body keeps the Score*, Viking

Van Manan, Max, 1990, *Researching Lived Experience*, Suny

Van der Kolk, Bessel, The neurobiology of childhood trauma and abuse; Child Adolescent Psychiatric Clinics N Am 12 (2003) 293–317

Weiss, J. Salomon and Sledon, H. Wagner, What Explains the Negative Consequences of Adverse Childhood Experiences on Adult Health; Insights from Cognitive and Neuroscience Research, American Journal of Preventive Medicine, 1998, 14 (4)

Wirtz, Ursula, 2014, *Trauma and Beyond*, Spring Journal Books

Wolkstein, Diana & Kramer, Samuel Noah, 1983; Innanna The Queen of Heaven, and Earth, Histories and Hymns from Sumer; Library of Congress

THANK YOU FOR READING THIS BOOK

If you would like to stay connected and receive or share more information please go to the website:

www.depthpsychologycenter.com

Or to the Facebook Page:
https://www.facebook.com/profile.php?id=61551763330999

Against All Odds

Made in United States
Troutdale, OR
01/07/2025